ROBERT WYETH

WHAT IS WRONG WITH SLAVERY

WORKBOOK PRESS LLC
187 E Warm Springs Rd,
Suite B285, Las Vegas, NV 89119, USA

Website: https://workbookpress.com/
Hotline: 1-888-818-4856
Email: admin@workbookpress.com

Ordering Information:
Quantity sales. Special discounts are available on quantity purchases by corporations, associations, and others.
For details, contact the publisher at the address above.

Library of Congress Control Number:

ISBN-13: 978-1-960752-05-5 (Paperback Version)
          978-1-960752-06-2 (Digital Version)

REV. DATE: 08/31/2022

What is Wrong with Slavery?

Robert Wyeth

If you had responded to my rebuke,
I would have poured out my heart to you
and made my thoughts known to you.
But since you rejected me when I called
and no-one gave heed when I stretched out my hand,
since you ignored all my advice
and would not accept my rebuke.
Proverbs ch.1 v23-25

Then they will call to me but I will not answer;
they will look for me but will not find me.
Since they hated knowledge
and did not choose to fear the Lord,
since they would not accept my advice
and spurned my rebuke.
Proverbs ch.1 v28-30

As a face is reflected in water,
so the heart reflects the real person.
Proverbs ch.27 v19 (NLT)

Contents

The New Testament

Acknowledgements

Most of the verses were taken from the NIV Bible:

The Holy Bible, New International Version ®, copyright 1973, 1978, 1984 by International Bible Society.
Copyright 1985 by the Zondervan Corporation.
Anglicisation 1987 by the Hodder and Stoughton Limited.

This edition first presented in Great Britain in 1987.

Other versions:

Holy Bible, New Living Translation ®, copyright © 1996, 2004 by Tyndale Charitable Trust, issued by the Tyndale House Publishers.

Summary

Slavery has been going on for a long while, probably it was always there. It was there in the Old Testament, the New Testament and still is going on today. It will be there until the conclusion of time when God judges the world.

In the Old Testament, God was mindful of the whole purpose of slavery. He delivered his people out of Egypt when they were slaves. Promised them a new start to life, in the Promised Land. But slavery continued as the Israelites moved about and considered the nations around them who had slaves. God promised that when the Israelites served him, slavery would be gone, but they didn't obey his commands. However, God made the Israelites slaves and should only serve for six years then be free again.

In the New Testament, under the Roman law the rich had slaves under them. In the church, there were indeed problems: how could a slave be free? What about the slave master? It was different now after Jesus had died bringing the kingdom of God back to those who had believed. Instead of being slaves to Satan doing evil things, we had to be slaves for God instead, doing righteous deeds.

That God had created man special like himself. He wanted man to be free from slavery and serve him, not to serve the devil.

God Exists

The Being of God

It is important to start with God, because he made man and woman in his image and his likeness. Mankind was the king over all the animals, the birds and the fish; he was there to protect the creatures that God had made. He selected mankind over all the other beings. He was special to God, he was even close to the Lord. Even in the garden God was there and he talked with Adam (see Genesis ch.3 v8-9).

Every human being is worthy of honour and respect. He can't be a slave looking after his master's affairs and business. Not looking to God as his good friend or companion.

Theism may be defined as the belief in the existence of God who creates and controls the world. There has not been an attempt at all to prove God lives and reigns. He would be there from Genesis to Revelation in the Bible which is our structure for living. It was assumed and nobody thought about it.

Today, when you go through the world, God is majestic, his greatness exceeds what man can do. Each person had an image of what God would be like. Though in a number of ways, when taken together, they can prove God's existence.

For example: God was:
Perfect.
Universal.
Design.
Selection.
Moral.
Religious.

Perfect: the concept of perfection and therefore that an absolutely perfect one must exist.

He is not served by human hands, as if he needed anything, because he himself gives all men life and breath and everything else. Acts ch.17 v25

Universal: the universe is not self-existent. Events are explained by the cause lying outside of them.

Who cuts a channel for the torrents of rain, and a path for the thunderstorm, to water a land where no man lives, a desert with no-one in it, to satisfy a desolate wasteland and make it sprout with grass? Job ch.38 v25-27

Design: there is an ordered design and consequently the design had a designer.

Who has understood the mind of the Lord, or instructed him as his counsellor? Whom did the Lord consult to enlighten him, who taught him the right way? Who was it that taught him knowledge or showed him the path of understanding? Isaiah ch.40 v13-14

Selection: there must be a greater personality, mind and will apart from man's existence.

Without faith ii is impossible to please God, because anyone who comes to him must believe he exists and that he rewards those who earnestly seek him. Hebrew ch.11 v6

Moral: the existence of someone who as lawgiver and judge has the absolute right to command man.

The wrath of God is being revealed from heaven against all the godliness and wickedness of men who suppress the truth by their wickedness, since what may be known about God is plain to them. Romans ch.1 v18-19

Religious: all the peoples and tribes of the earth there is a sense of the divine, that naturally leads to religious worship of many kinds.

They tell how you turned to God from idols to serve the living and true God. 1 Thessalonians ch.1 v9

Other Rivals of God

There are some who maintain that God in his wisdom might may not exist at all, for example:

Agnosticism.
Atheism.
Deism.
Pantheism.
Polytheism.

Agnosticism: this declares that God is unknowable and underlines the moral government of God. He hands something to someone else.

Atheism: this a denial of God, that the universe is 'self-sufficient', whatever that means.

Deism: this means that there is a powerful God but separates him from man; he removes God from his own universe or existence.

Pantheism: this describes the universe as a 'phase of God' who is reduced to a mere man.

Polytheism: this has a belief in the plurality of God; there is more than one God.

In the whole Bible, God has always been taken to represent the supreme being. The world exists only because God maintains and nurtures it (see Psalm 139).

These things are error and would be taken as man trying to forget his creator.

Sin is there and man cannot face God alone. However, after death man has to face the judgement of God. There is no justification for any mistakes that humans have to give. The Bible is what counts as the truth, and it is the whole truth.

For we will all stand before God's judgement seat. It is written: "As surely as I live," says the Lord, "Every knee will bow before me; every tongue will confess to God." So then, each of us will give an account of himself to God. Romans ch.14 v10-12

Each person will come to face God and the man-made, basic errors will be cast aside. Every knee will bow to the Lord and every tongue will confess him as he is God. There is no excuse, young or old, rich or poor, slave or free.

The Nature of God

God exists but we don't see him. We pretend that we don't see God but his work is there for any one to see.

Since what may be known about God is plain to them. Romans ch.1 v19

The fool says in his heart, "There is no God." They are corrupt, their deeds are vile; there is no-one who does good. Psalm ch.14 v1

The chair we are sitting on, we don't check that the wood is solid, the joints are held tight, we sit down without thinking about it. This is faith and we do it time and time again. We are comfortable with faith. What about the aeroplane and the ship, do we check before entering? Of course not, we rely on the engineers and the supervision who constructed them.

We must have faith to trust in God.

The Lord looks down from heaven on the sons of men to see if there are any who understand, any who seek God. Psalm ch.14 v2

It is the reason why we read the Bible, to seek and search out God. In the Scriptures, God has certain attributes, or he has traits or characteristics of his personality. This is important when he created or made man.

For example, the natural attributes:
Infinity.
Inclusive.
Eternal.
Universal.
All-knowing.
Supremacy.

Infinity: God is limitless. He was there at the beginning and he will be at the end when God judges man.

Jesus was with God in the beginning. John ch.1 v2

Inclusive: the personality in God. Mind, emotions, will and freedom it is all there.

In him we were also chosen, having been predestined according to the plan of him who works out everything in conformity with the purpose of his will. Ephesians ch.1 v11

Eternal: that God is eternal and changeless.

Now to the King eternal, immortal, invisible, the only God, be honour and glory for every and ever. Amen. 1 Timothy ch.1 v17

Universal: his detachment as self-existent from his creatures and his nearness to everything else.

So that in everything he might have the supremacy. Colossians ch.1 v18

All-knowing: God's knowledge is part of his own nature. God knows the future, the past and he possesses foreknowledge.

He hands nations over to him and subdues kings before him ... who has done this and carried it through, calling forth the generations from the beginning? I, the Lord - with the first of them and with the last - I am he. Isaiah ch.41 v2, v4

Supremacy: God's power does not extend to anything which is self-contradictory. He frequently uses ordinary measures, like healing diseases or weather patterns.

That our Lord is greater than all gods. The Lord does whatever pleases him, in the heavens and on the earth, in the seas and all their depths. He makes clouds rise from the ends of the earth; he sends lightning with the rain and brings out the wind from his storehouses. Psalm ch.135 v5-7

And the moral attributes:

> Goodness.
> Holiness.
> Righteousness.

Goodness: God continually seeks the welfare of his creation.

The Lord loves righteousness and justice; the earth is full of his unfailing love. Psalm ch.33 v5

Holiness: the separation from all that is impure which is limited and imperfect.

I will not carry out my fierce anger, nor will I turn and devastate Ephraim. For I am God, and not man - the Holy One among you. I will not come in wrath. Hosea ch.11 v9

For it is written: "Be holy, because I am holy." 1 Peter ch.1 v16

Righteousness: righteousness, justice, truth and anger is what God is like. His nature to be righteous and it is impossible for him to act otherwise.

The Lord works righteousness and justice for all the oppressed. Psalm ch.103 v6

God Is Spirit

Jesus talked with a Samaritan woman. He was tired from his journey and sat down by the well while his disciples went to get some food. A Samaritan woman in the heat of the day came to draw water. She was not liked because of her marriage customs, basically all the Samaritans don't like the Jews (see John ch.4 v9).

Jesus said, God Is spirit, and his worshippers must worship in spirit and in truth. John ch.4 v24

The Samaritan woman didn't understand what Jesus meant by, 'God is spirit'. He is trying to convince the woman that God can be in any place that he wants and even here by the well.

- - - - - - - - - - - - -

Abraham was sitting in his tent in the heat of the day and it was hot.

Abraham looked up and saw three men, standing nearby. When he saw them, he hurried from the entrance of his tent to meet them and bowed low to the ground. Genesis ch.18 v2

The figures that God used was three men, looking like any other men but Abraham didn't notice. He bowed low to the ground. He politely addressed them as 'my lords' called himself 'your servant' (see Genesis ch.19 v2). It was a common way of speaking when addressing superiors, because he was pleased that they had come to his house.

Then the Lord said, "The outcry against Sodom and Gomorrah is so great and their sin so grievous that I will go down and see if what they have done is as bad as the outcry that has reached me. If not, I will know. Geneses ch.18 v20-21

God is spirit, pure, personal and infinite which means that he can be all round the world and doesn't have to be like a man. Not only that, he can travel anywhere he likes. The stars give some understanding what he can do. He can be anywhere and everywhere. Even the billions of stars in the universe, that man has come to accept and the universe is so big, so large.

- - - - - - - - - - - - -

Jesus said, "For the Son of Man came to seek and save what was lost." Luke ch.19 v10

He was talking about Zacchaeus a chief tax collector who was wealthy and he gave the Romans the taxes, but kept some for himself. The people didn't like him because he gave the tax over to the Romans. He rounded up the people and said, 'You must pay the taxes to the authorities'.

Every one was lost not the chief tax collector, but everybody. Jesus came to look for the lost. That will be true in the New Testament times and it is still true today. He is still there in heaven, but he is looking for the lost. This is why he doesn't appear in the sky to come back. He is looking at you.

God is spirit and is looking for the lost to save them from hell. So, when God judges the world, the bad and evil persons go to hell.

Purpose of Slaves

Man in his Image

His heavenly court consisted of the angels to announce his work to the members of his heavenly court. Who were there first before the earth was created? When the earth was made the angels were there to sing the praises of their creator?

Where were you when I laid the earth's foundation? ... On what were its footings set, or who laid its cornerstone - while the morning stars sang together and all the angels shouted for joy? Job ch.38 v4, v6-7

The angels came before mankind.

Then God said, "Let us make man in our image, in our likeness, and let them rule over the fish in the sea and the birds of the air, over the livestock, over all the earth, and over the creatures that move along the ground." Genesis ch.1 v26

What does that mean?

Image: is a portrait of a person, a person that closely represents another.

Likeness: to have fondness or affection and satisfaction with others.

No distinction should be made between 'image' and 'likeness' which are synonyms in both the Old Testament (see Genesis ch.5 v1 and ch.9 v6) and the New Testament (see 1 Corinthians ch.11 v7; Colossians ch.3 v10; James ch.3 v9). Image includes such characteristics as righteousness and holiness (see Ephesians ch.4 v24), and knowledge (see Colossians ch.3 v10). It relates to a likeness of Christ (see Romans ch.8 v29).

It is really is the same thought, image and likeness go together.

So God created man in his own image, in the image of God he created him; make and female he created them. Genesis ch.1 v27

Since man was created in God's image, he delegated authority over to man and he ruled all of the creatures that God had created. God made man in his image and it is not good for him to be a slave working for his master. He was a slave the same as his master; all were created by God himself.

There is no slave or slavery. Each person was unique, every one is special to God.

Slaves and Slavery

What happened when slaves were formed?

The fall of man and woman made a considerable difference to the world, not only to the earth, but to the whole of the solar system right to the extent of the stars. Red giants and white dwarfs, stars come and go this is not what God created.

God said, "Cursed is the ground because of you; through painful toil you will eat of it all the days of your life" ... the Lord God made garments of skin for Adam and his wife and clothed them. Genesis ch.3 v17, v21

Man would have to die, so the animals and all creation will have to die as well. Including all the stars, planets and suns. It is the whole universe together. Sin is wilfully going against God and the whole creation is marred and spoiled.

God said, "It will produce thorns and thistles for you." Genesis ch.3 v18

For the creation was subjected to frustration, not by its own choice, but by the will of the one who subjected it. In hope that the creation itself will be liberated from its bondage to decay and bought in to the glorious freedom of the children of God. Romans ch.8 v20-21

Adam and Eve brought about by sin what we can see today. Each one will die including all the stars, animals on the ground, birds in the air, fish in the sea, trees and plants and even mankind. It will be the same until God rescues it. We will be locked into the world; it will get worse not better.

Current thinking if the world will get better and illness would be passed away. That is not the Bible view. It maintains the earth will deteriorate, degenerate and go into decline and end up in a fireball (see 2 Peter ch.3 v7-12).

Slave is the word used for a person:
> To be kept as property for a master.
> Made to work as a servant.
> Submissively under domination.
> Who has lost lower of resistance.
> Who works extremely hard.
> There's no wages for the effort caused.

There is no evidence that God made anyone work as a slave. Every one is precious to God.

So, what happened?

God Floods the Earth

Now the earth was corrupt in God's sight and was full of violence. God saw how corrupt the earth had become, for all the people of earth had corrupted their ways. Genesis ch.6 v11-12

Slavery was still there in the people. One is rich and the other is poor, the poor people belong to the rich. It is still slavery. It was acceptable for man to be 'full of violence' among anybody and everybody. So, God removed all the people from their land where they lived. All the animals and creatures by flooding the earth with water from below and above. But Noah and his family stayed in the ark and several animals and birds stayed with them.

The waters flooded the earth for a hundred and fifty days. Genesis ch.7 v24

God said, "Never again will I curse the ground because of man, even though every inclination of his heart is evil from childhood. And never again will I destroy all the living creatures, as I have done." Genesis ch.8 v21

The flooding is not possible to destroy man and the living creatures.

By these waters also the world of that time was deluged and destroyed. By the same word the present heaven and earth are reserved for fire, being kept for the day of judgement and destruction of ungodly men. 2 Peter ch.3 v6-7

Then God will cause the world to be by fire, covering everything. Earth and sky will be consumed by fire. God doesn't change. If the world as its current system was as bad as in the days of Noah by evil and violence, God will react the same way by total fire.

- - - - - - - - - - -

When the flood had finished, Noah became drunk with his wine.

Noah, a man of the soil, proceeded to plant a vineyard. When he drank some of its wine, he became drunk and lay uncovered inside his tent. Genesis ch.9 v20-21

Ham the father of Canaan discovered his father drunk, he did not to as his brothers' did, by covering him with a blanket, walking backwards. So Noah said to his youngest son when he recovered from his drunkenness:

Cursed be Canaan! the lowest of slaves will be to his brothers. Genesis ch.9 v25

God had removed all of the sin and the violence of the people. Noah was drunk and he pronounced him a slave to his other brothers. So will be the slave. This is the first time in the Bible where slavery is mentioned. Noah cursed his son and slaves will always be there when the flood is ended.

That is why the rich had slaves to work for them.

The Final End

The apostle John was in Patmos, shut up on a desolate isle because of the word of God. It was on the Lord's Day and he saw a vision. He saw another angel coming down from heaven with a mighty voice he said:

"Babylon the Great also bought cinnamon, spice, incense, myrrh, frankincense, wine, olive oil, fine flour, wheat, cattle, sheep, horses, chariots, and bodies—that is, human slaves." Revelation ch.18 v13 (NLT)

When the kings of the earth who shared Babylon's luxury. They will weep and mourn over her, the merchants and sea, captains who sold their slave cargoes any more. Slaves will still be there at the end of time.

"Come! Gather together for the great banquet God has prepared. Come and eat the flesh of kings, generals, and strong warriors; of horses and their riders; and of all humanity, both free and slave, small and great." Revelation ch.19 v17-18 (NLT)

John saw heaven open, there was a white horse whose rider was called 'Faithful and True'. With justice he judges and makes war. The 'free and slave' will be there and they will be destroyed by the angel and his armies (see Revelation ch.19 v11-21).

This is the last time that slaves will be mentioned in the Bible. From start to finish, slavery will be there throughout all the generations because sin is present in the people from Adam and Eve. They passed it on as we are all children for the generations to come.

From Noah to the end of time, you can't stop slaves being there. The rich and the poor, the slaves being the poor and who work for the rich.

The Old Testament

Slaves Under Abraham

As the sun was setting, Abram fell into a deep sleep, and a thick and dreadful darkness came over him. Then the Lord said to him, "Know for certain that your descendants will be strangers in a foreign country not their own, and they will be enslaved and ill-treated four hundred years. But I will punish the nation they serve as slaves, and afterwards they will come out with great possessions." Genesis ch.15 v12-14

Abram (God named him in Abraham) was in a sleep, but not a nightmare where things might happen. The sun was going down and God told him, 'Your offspring will be slaves and badly ill-treated, strangers away from here in the Promised Land.' This caused Abram to be frightened and worried by the things that will certainly happen.

The Lord said, "In the fourth generation your descendants will come back here, for the sin of the Amorites has not reached its full measure." Genesis ch.15 v16

'The Amorites in the Promised Land have not experienced their full capacity for evil, so when they do', God said, 'I will wipe them out and destroy them'. The sinful Canaanite religious practices were known from the archaeological artefacts and from their own literature. Their worship was polytheistic (many gods) and included child sacrifice, idolatry, religious prostitution and divination.

It will be a long time, for over 400 generations. They carried on with what their fathers had been doing, a man-made, horrible tradition and it was evil and bad.

Joseph a Slave

Joseph was the eleventh son of Jacob and his favourite son. A boy sold into slavery by his jealous brothers. He was cast into prison for failing to obey Potipher's wife. He rose to the highest state under Pharaoh because he recalled his dream and explained what will happen. He was clever enough to avoid the famine for the whole region of Egypt

The king's chief cup-bearer spoke to Pharaoh who had a dream.

There was a young Hebrew man with us in the prison who was a slave of the captain of the guard. We told him our dreams, and he told us what each of our dreams meant. And everything happened just as he had predicted. I was restored to my position as cup-bearer, and the chief baker was executed and impaled on a pole." Genesis ch.41 v12-13 (NLT)

Pharaoh rescued Joseph from prison and he was elected to help with the famine. When Joseph's brothers went to Egypt to buy grain, Joseph noticed them, but they didn't expect to see him in his robes and authority. Dressed like an Egyptian.

I am Joseph, your brother, whom you sold into slavery in Egypt. But don't be upset, and don't be angry with yourselves for selling me to this place. It was God who sent me here ahead of you to preserve your lives. Genesis ch.45 v4-5 (NLT)

He understood that it was God who sent Joseph to Egypt for the period before the famine, it lasted seven brutal years all the famine was in Egypt and Palestine.

Why were the brothers jealous? (see Genesis ch.37 v2-11)
Joseph a young man of seventeen.

Was herding sheep for his father, Jacob.
He brought his father a bad report about his brothers.
Jacob loved Joseph more than any of his sons.
He had been born to him in his old age.
He made a richly ornamental cloak for him.
Joseph had two dreams:
>   His brothers sheave bowing down to Joseph's sheaf of corn.
>   Sun and moon and eleven stars were bowing down to Joseph.

When Joseph's brothers saw that their father was dead, they said, "What if Joseph holds a grudge against us and pays us back for all the wrongs, we did to him?" Genesis ch.50 v15

The brothers became anxious and worried when Joseph was in charge of the famine. He was married and had Manasseh and Ephraim by Asenath, the daughter of Potiphera, priest of On (see Genesis ch.46 v20).

His brothers then came and threw themselves down before him. "We are your slaves," they said. Genesis ch.50 v18

It was hard to forget long ago what his brothers did to Joseph. They ignored him and thought he was dead. They had to remember that they were in Egypt under Joseph's power and influence, but not Joseph's slaves.

Israelites Oppressed

Jacob and his family moved into Egypt to see Joseph and he lived for seventeen years (see Genesis ch.47 v28). The Israelites settled in the region of Goshen. For all shepherds are detestable to the Egyptians (see Genesis ch.46 v31-34). Goshen is a place well away from what the Egyptians were doing near the River Nile.

Then a new king (Pharaoh) came to power in Egypt, but he did not know about Joseph and the famine; it was in the past (see Exodus ch.1 v8-11). He said about the Israelites who were increasing rapidly:

      We must deal shrewdly with them.

      They will become even more numerous.

      If war break out they will join our enemies.

      Fight against us and leave our country.

So the Egyptians made the Israelites their slaves. They appointed brutal slave drivers over them, hoping to wear them down with crushing labour. They forced them to build the cities of Pithom and Rameses as supply centres for the king. But the more the Egyptians oppressed them, the more the Israelites multiplied and spread, and the more alarmed the Egyptians became. So the Egyptians worked the people of Israel without mercy. They made their lives bitter, forcing them to mix mortar and make bricks and do all the work in the fields. They were ruthless in all their demands. Exodus ch.1 v11-14 (NLT)

It is not surprising that the Egyptian masters would have been worried about the many Israelite families. If the Canaanites and the Philistines wanted to attack Egypt. There were two roads leading into Palestine from the land of Goshen and it would be easier to pass through. It was the entrance to Egypt to avoid all the desert regions.

God said, "I will surely raise my hand against them so that their slaves will plunder them." Zechariah ch.2 v9

Why did the Israelites become slaves?
>They were in a foreign country, not their own land.
>They might have preferred Egypt rather than Palestine.
>There was the Lake Menzaleh passing through Goshen.
>The grass was growing richly through the lake.
>Rather than being in the hill-country in Palestine.
>They were shepherds and had many flocks.

Diligent hands will rule, but laziness ends in slave labour. Proverbs ch.12 v24

But they didn't fight back and accepted being slaves under the Egyptians. But God knew about it and he mentioned the slaves to Abraham.

The Passover

When the Lord struck the Egyptians with a number of plagues. During the night on the last plague, Israel was ejected from the land of Egypt including all the flocks and herds.

The Egyptians got up during the night; and there was a loud wailing in Egypt, for there was not a house without someone dead. Exodus ch.12 v30

At midnight the Lord struck down all the firstborn in Egypt, from the Pharaoh to the prisoner in the dungeon.

On the Passover, the Israelite families would each take a lamb and put blood on the sides and tops of the door. During the night, the Lord will avoid every house where the blood will be a sign for the Israelites. The blood is what God looked for, what provided safety for those who sheltered beneath it in their houses. It is the blood of an animal that the Israelites had sinned, the lamb had to be killed.

"These are the regulations for the Passover: No foreigner is to eat of it, any slave you have brought may eat of it after you have circumcised him, but a temporary resident or a hired worker may not eat of it." Exodus ch.12 v43-45

No uncircumcised slave may eat of it, but only slaves who had been consecrated to the Lord. It means that the slave had to be holy to set apart to be a holy, devoted person.

The whole community of Israel must celebrate it. Exodus ch.12 v47

The Israelites had to sacrifice to God for their sins the blood of an animal.

In fact, the law requires that nearly everything be cleansed with blood, and without the shedding of blood there is no forgiveness. Hebrews ch.9 v22

When Jesus came, he sacrificed his blood on the cross to save us. The blood is the key for us to come to God. It was the blood that made an atonement, to appease God himself (see Romans ch.3 v25 and 1 Peter ch.1 v19-20).

The Israelites were indeed slaves: (see Exodus ch.12 v32-36)
> The had houses to live in.
> They had flocks and herds.
> There was articles of silver and gold to collect.
> There was much clothing.
> They plundered the Egyptians when they left.

Hebrew Slave Must be Freed

They entered the Desert of Sinai, and Israel camped there in the desert in front of the mountain. Exodus ch.19 v2

The journey of the Israelites from Goshen came to Mount Sinai. Located in the region of the Wilderness of Paran, going south for about 200 miles from where they stayed by the Mediterranean Sea. It was a long way down along by the Reed Sea. There they met with God.

Then Moses went up to God, and the Lord called to him from the mountain. Exodus ch.19 v3

He gave Moses the Ten Commandments and laws to help with the exiled Israelites. All of them were slaves and they were used to the Egyptians calling out to them and giving them instructions. They were not used to being alone. This was an important lesson they must decide for themselves.

If you buy a Hebrew servant; he is to serve you for six years. But in the seventh year, he shall go free, without paying anything. Exodus ch.21 v2

Why? Because if you have worked the slave hard for more than six years the poor slave wouldn't have a chance to get free. The Lord banned the wealth of property and possessions to disadvantage the poor. He was concerned about those who didn't have anything.

Because the Israelites are my servants, whom I brought out of Egypt, they must not be sold as slaves. Do not rule over them ruthlessly; but fear your God. Your male and female slaves are to come from the nations around you; from them you may buy slaves. Leviticus ch.25 v42-44

The Lord's servants are not to be anyone's perpetual slave. This an abuse of what God intended in his image. Particularly, the Israel must show that they cared for the slave. For they were once, ill-treated slaves.

The land must not be sold permanently, because the land is mine and you are but aliens and my tenants. Leviticus ch.25 v23

The land is God's (but we forget that; we have a freehold over our property). The Israelites are but tenants working for the Lord and there is no room for slaves. Each one had a duty to work for the Lord.

Rich and poor have this in common: the Lord is the Maker of them all. Proverbs ch.22 v2

Whether we are rich or poor we are only there because God wants us to be here on this earth. We have a job to do.

Sells his Daughter as a Slave

When a man sells his daughter as a slave, she will not be freed at the end of six years as the men are. Exodus ch.21 v7 (NLT)

The rights of a wife and her daughter are not the same as today. The man had full control over his daughter and did what he desired. He could marry her and she had not the right to protest. Consider Jephthah the Gidianite, who was a mighty warrior and fought against the Ammonite king.

Jephthah made a vow to the Lord: "If you give the Ammonites into my hands, whatever comes out of door of my house to meet me when I return in triumph from the Ammonites will be the Lord's, and I will sacrifice it as a burnt offering." Judges ch.11 v30-31

When Jephthah returned to his house who should come out of his house but his daughter and he did what he said he would do. It was a vow to the Lord.

This is what the Lord commands: When a man makes a vow to the Lord or takes an oath to bind himself by a pledge; he must not break his word but must do everything he said. Numbers ch.30 v1-2

Jesus said, "But I tell you, do not swear at all: either by heaven, for it is God's throne; or by the earth, for it is his footstool; or by Jerusalem, for it is the city of the Great King. Do not swear by your head, for you cannot make even one hair white or black. Simply let your 'Yes' be 'Yes', and your 'No', No'; anything beyond this comes from the evil one." Matthew ch.5 v34-37

It is the same as in the New Testament. Do not make a vow to God, whether by practice or in front of everybody. Otherwise, it will come from the devil, or Satan. You do not know in the future what things you might be faced with. It is important that if you make a vow to the Lord, you will have to do it.

However, when a man sells his daughter as a slave. She is not to do the things that a grown man had done, with power and strength. She is to be treated as a woman.

The slave master will decide: (see Exodus ch.21 v7-11)
    He has selected her for himself as a wife.
    He has no right to sell her to some foreigners who want her.
    If he selects her for his son.
    He must grant her the rights of a daughter.
    He must give her food, clothing and marital rights.
    She is free to go without any payment of money.

That is why she must not be released after six years: she is his daughter and not a slave.

Death of a Slave

The duties of a slave who is bound to his slave master who directs him and controls him. There are four things which in the law of Moses that God commanded the slave master to do:

If a man beats his slave with a rod.

If a man hits his slave in the eye.

If a man knocks out the tooth of a slave.

If a bull gores a slave.

A rod: if a master beats his male or female slave with a rod, the master has to be punished, but not if the slave gets up and is not dead. A sound thrashing is acceptable, but not to kill the slave. If he gets up after a day or two and survives.

"If a man beats his male or female slave with a rod and the slave dies as a direct result, he must be punished, but he is not to be punished if the slave gets up a day or two, since the slave is his property." Exodus ch.21 v20-21

Eye and tooth: if a slave master attacks the slave and the eye is blinded or he knocks out the tooth he must let the slave go free.

"If a man hits his male or female slave in the eye and the eye is blinded, he must let the slave go free to compensate for the eye. And if a man knocks out the tooth of his male or female slave, he must let the slave go free to compensate for the tooth." Exodus ch.21 v26-27 (NLT)

Within the six years that a slave must serve his master.

The bull: if a bull is penned up, but goes to attack a slave, the owner of the bull must pay the master and the bull must die. There is no remedy for the male or female slave. He or she must live with the consequences.

If the bull gores a male or female slave, the owner must pay thirty shekels of silver to the master of the slave, and the bull must be stoned. Exodus ch.21 v32

You can see the difference: If you beat the slave with a rod or let the bull gore him, it is just and reasonable, but not if he dies. But if a slave is blinded in one eye or a tooth is knocked out then he can go free. The master has control over the slave but not if he attacks him ruthlessly. The rod is a painful exercise it might certainly lead to death of the slave.

Most other people in the nations around them, they would treat a slave with brutality and treat him as worthy of physical abuse. God instructed his people to be not like that. The slave master ruthlessly takes it out with a slave both male and female. It was physical and malicious where by a slave master could treat his slaves like that, but not if they died as a result of their punishment. The slave master ruled over his slave.

Thief Will be a Slave

A thief who is caught must pay in full for everything he stole. If he cannot pay, he must be sold as a slave to pay for his theft. Exodus ch.22 v3 (NLT)

God did not intend his people to have nothing to give. All the sacrificial offerings at the temple required an animal or a bird to go to the priest.

If the offering to the Lord is a burnt offering of birds, he is to offer a dove or a young pigeon. Leviticus ch.1 v14

Or, if he didn't have anything like sheep, an offering of a bird might be acceptable.

If he cannot afford a lamb, he is to present two doves or two young pigeons to the Lord as a penalty for his sin - one for a sin offering and the other as a burnt offering. Leviticus ch.5 v7

When a person sins, he will be surely be accountable to God. Like:
   A public charge to testify to something he knew.
   He touches an unclean animal.
   He touches any human uncleanness.
   He makes an oath to do anything.

That is a lot, throughout the day. Everybody must present to the Lord something. This is a sacrifice of sin. Everybody sins, whether they think it so or not.

The year of the tithe, you shall give it to the Levite, the alien, the fatherless and the widow, so that they may eat it in your towns and be satisfied. Deuteronomy ch.26 v12

Be sure to set aside a tenth of all that your fields produce each year. Deuteronomy ch.14 v22

This means that you have to give a tithe, an offering of something like animal, grain or fruit from your land. What your fields produce each year. It is an offering each year to the Lord.

This is what you must give to the Lord as a tithe:
>   The Levite, who doesn't have a share in God's land.
>   The alien who wanders about looking for a place to live.
>   The fatherless and the widow who looks to God for help.
>   The tithe to give to God in his temple.

Moses said, "He brought us to this place and gave us this land, a land flowing with milk and honey; and now I bring the firstfruits of the soil that you, O Lord, have given me." Deuteronomy ch.26 v9-10

God didn't say thieve or snatch or take what is not yours. This is one of the Ten Commandments that the Lord your God gave you:

You shall not steal. Exodus ch.20 v15

This is why an Israelite must be held accountable to God and go into slavery because he didn't have anything to pay back. Nothing of value, no job to get payment for, no fields to get plenty. Not even honey that you could use from the fields to offer.

Lazy hands make a man poor, but diligent hands bring wealth. Proverbs ch.10 v4

It would be totally lazy, work-shy and good-for-nothing, to have an Israelite who did not work. That is why the thief who does not think of anything but himself will go into slavery. The Israelite should not steal and break down the whole community. That is why it is wrong.

On the Sabbath

God made the entire solar system. The lights in the sky (sun, moon and the stars), the plants, the animals, the birds and the fish in only one week. Don't be startled or alarmed, thinking that the world was created billions of years ago. God made everything in 6 days, this is the power and might of God.

But why did the Israelites have the seventh day as a day of rest? Each week we have the Sabbath and the Israelites knew that God rested on the Sabbath, and that the people should do the same. From the beginning to the end, each Israelite man or woman had to rest on the Sabbath day. One day a week, because God created everything in one week.

By the seventh day God had finished the work he had been doing; so on the seventh day he rested from all his work. And God blessed the seventh day and made it holy, because on it he rested from all the work of creating that he had done. Genesis ch.2 v2-3

He was not tired like us, nor weary about what he had been doing.

God said, "Six days do your work, but on the seventh day do not work, so that your ox and your donkey may rest and the slave born in your household, and the alien as well, may be refreshed." Exodus ch.23 v12

It is a time for rest, a time for leisure and relaxation.

For in six days the Lord made the heavens and the earth, the sea, and all that is in them, but he rested on the seventh day. Therefore, the Lord blessed the Sabbath day and made it holy. Exodus ch.20 v11

This is one of the Ten Commandments that the Lord your God gave for the Israelites. Even the slaves rested each week on the Sabbath day. God reminded his people that they needed to take time off from what they had been doing. To lie-down and sleep to have a measure of calm in the activities in which they did their jobs and their work.

God didn't need to rest; he was indeed Spirit:

If it were his intention and he withdrew his spirit and breath, all mankind would perish together and man would return to the dust. Job ch.34 v14-15

He held the 'universe in his hands' and God made sure that all would be well and that the earth would exist until the end of time. Every week, God made sure that the slave would be well enough to work through the week. It is important to rest for one day out of the week. We have forgotten that in our everyday life, it's important to rest and relax. We are reminded for the process and work we should be doing it all the week.

God reminded us that it was important to take time off and even slaves.

Sex With a Slave Girl

If another male has sex with a slave girl and is found out or discovered, she is committed to her master for ever, promising to him for life. But her freedom has never been purchased. The master hasn't decided what to do with her.

If a man has sex with a slave girl whose freedom has never been purchased but who is committed to become another man's wife, he must pay full compensation to her master. But since she is not a free woman, neither the man nor the woman will be put to death. The man, however, must bring a ram as a guilt offering and present it to the Lord at the entrance of the Tabernacle. The priest will then purify him before the Lord with the ram of the guilt offering, and the man's sin will be forgiven. Leviticus ch.19 v20-22 (NLT)

A slave girl is the property of her master, she doesn't have the right to protest about it, only the guilty man must come before the priest to make amends for his sin. It is a ram as a guilt offering, he must take it to the priest and the guilty man's sin will be forgiven. Neither the man or woman must be put to death.

There is no evidence of what the slave girl should be doing, but her master would keep her safe within his family. Her master might not take her for his partner, but keep her as a slave for his son. If the woman had been free and not slave girl, death would have been enforced, for example:

If a man happens to meet in a town a virgin pledged to be married and he sleeps with her, you shall take both of them to the gate of that town and stone them to death - the girl because she was in a town and did not scream for help ... If out in the country a man happens to meet a girl pledged to be married and rapes her, only the man who has done this shall die. Deuteronomy ch.22 v23-25

One who is entrusted and is going to be married soon, a virgin. A man takes her and rapes her. This is one of the Ten Commandments that the

Lord your God gave you:

You shall not commit adultery. Exodus ch.20 v14

Adultery: is where voluntary sexual intercourse between a married person and someone who is not their legal partner, or fornication where voluntary sexual intercourse between unmarried people.

What About the Kidnapper?

If a person attacks another, kidnaps him, overrides him and sells him as a slave.

Kidnappers must be put to death, whether they are caught in possession of their victims or have already sold them as slaves. Exodus ch.21 v16 (NLT)

A kidnapper must be put to death, regardless of the circumstances. Whether an Israelite or another person in the nearby countries around the Promised Land. Kidnapping is a truly horrible thing; it will take a person's life away and therefore the penalty is death by stoning.

You will have to be sure that it is right and we will have judges who can pronounce the verdict.

The law is not clear whether the slaves are free to go, what will happen to the person who receives the slaves, without knowing it. However, anyway, after the Year of Jubilee the slaves must go back to their homes. If it is an Israelite, they must only serve six years.

Kidnapping must be dealt with whereas he would abduct or capture a hostage, someone would know about it. God would write it in his books and when the judgement comes the kidnapper will come to face God and suffer the condemnation (see Revelation ch.20 v12).

Priest Buys a Slave

Even the priests may buy a male and female slave. The priests share of food came from the Israelites. They were sacred and the food they were offered was holy. The priests had duty in the service of the Lord so they could not go out to tend the sheep, neither could they bring in the crops to harvest while they were working on the land. They had a duty to serve God in his temple.

But what about the slave who is bound by a priest?

If the priest buys a slave for himself, the slave may eat from the sacred offerings. And if his slaves have children, they also may share his food. Leviticus ch.22 v11 (NLT)

So the law of God makes this possible:
        The priest buys a male and female slave.
        They were permitted to eat from the priests sacred offerings.
        If slaves have children born in the priest's house.
        They also may also share his food.

Only if they were the priest's slaves and didn't run away, they were allowed to eat with the family. But if they departed and ran away, they were on their own and could not share his food because the food was holy.

Year of Jubilee

This is God's requirement due to the land. After six years of sowing, pruning and gathering, the Promised Land should lay fallow for one year. If the field grew wild, it was for the poor and all the wild animals to feast themselves properly, without the risk of people coming out and tending the soil. Scaring the animals and people away from the land.

I will send you such a blessing in the sixth year that the land will yield enough for three years. While you plant during the eighth year, you will eat from the old crop and will continue to eat from it until the harvest of the ninth year comes in. Leviticus ch.25 v21-22

When the seventh year came round, the Israelites were assured by the Lord that he would provide enough food for them. For the current year, the year of Jubilee and the year after that.

Consecrate the fiftieth year and proclaim liberty throughout the land to all its inhabitants. It shall be a Jubilee for you; each one is to return to his family property and each to his own clan ... For it is a Jubilee and is to be holy for you; eat only what is taken directly from the fields. Leviticus ch.25 v10, v12

Then the jubilee: (see Leviticus ch.25 v23-55)
    If you sell land to one of your countrymen.
    The land must not be sold permanently.
    If one of your countryman becomes poor.
    His nearest relative is to come to redeem it from him.
    If a man sells a house in a walled city.
    If it is not redeemed for a whole year.
    The house shall belong permanently to the buyer.
    If a man become poor.
    You must not take interest or sell him food at a profit.
    Do not make him work as a slave.

He is to be treated as a hired worker.

Why?

In the seventh year the land is to have a Sabbath of rest, a Sabbath to the Lord ... The land is to have a year of rest. Leviticus ch.25 v4-5

If the land was used for growing vegetables including wheat, the Israelites didn't have any rotation plan (like today). They didn't have crops that used up different materials from the soil. If you keep planting in the same plot the soil will become depleted of nitrogen and the plants will become sick. This is why God made a plan for the Jubilee, every six years we had one year when it is fallow and nothing could grow in the field. The soil and the worms could go back to start again becoming good for the next 6 years.

God was in control over the land so he decided that the land shall lie fallow. The Israelites didn't even know that.

Slaves From the Nations

God maintained that the Israelites must not be hired as slaves.

The people of Israel are my servants, whom I brought out of Egypt, they must not be sold as slaves ... but you must not rule over your fellow Israelites ruthlessly. Leviticus ch.25 v42, v46

However, you may purchase slaves from the nations around you. From them you may buy slaves:
>Slaves bought in from captivity, when you fight against the people.
>Alien and temporary residents born in your country.
>You will give them to your children as inherited property.
>You may make them slaves for life.

If one of your countryman became poor among you and sells himself to you, do not make him work as a slave. Leviticus ch.25 v39

Even if he is not redeemed in any of these ways, he and his children are to be released in the Year of Jubilee, for the Israelite belongs to me as servants. Leviticus ch.25 v54-55

If an Israelite man becomes poor and sells himself to the alien living among you or to a member of the alien's clan: (see Leviticus ch.25 v35-43)
>He retains the right of redemption.
>One of his relatives may redeem himself.
>If he becomes rich, he may redeem himself.
>But only until the Year of Jubilee.
>He is to be treated a man hired from year to year

Only the Israelite slaves and their children are to be released in the Year of Jubilee.

I am the Lord your God, who brought you out of Egypt so that you would no longer be slaves to the Egyptians; I broke the bars of your yoke and enabled you to walk with heads held high. Leviticus ch.26 v13

God instructed them not to let the poor Israelite be slaves. To do everything else to make them self-sufficient and work hard. But not the nations around them.

Temple Slaves

The Lord declares a holy war against the Midianites as one of Moses last actions before the end of his life.

The plunder remaining from the spoils that the soldiers took was 675,000 sheep, 72,000 cattle, 61,000 donkeys and 32,000 woman who had never slept with a man ... From the Israelites half, Moses selected one out of every fifty persons and animals, as the Lord commanded him, and gave them to the Levites, who were responsible for the care of the Lord's tabernacle. Numbers ch.31 v32, v47

Why was that necessary?

For the Midianites part in seducing Israel to engage in sexual immorality and to worship the Baal of Peor (see Numbers ch.25 v16-18). It was he last thing to eject the Israelites going into the Promised Land and wilfully corrupting the will of God, especially with coupled with the Balaam prophecies:

To the teaching of Balaam, who taught to entice the Israelites to sin by eating food sacrificed to idols and by committing sexual immorality. Revelation ch.2 v14

It is the practise of the Levite, to be ready to remove the tabernacle from where it was going. To take it down, to transport it and even put it up and the Midianite slaves would help with this work.

Now Eli, who was very old, heard about everything his sons were doing to all Israel and how they slept with the women who served at the entrance to the Tent of Meeting. So he said to them, "Why do you do such things? I hear from all the people about these wicked deeds of yours." 1 Samuel ch.2 v22-23

Ritual prostitution: the practice of ritual prostitution was an important feature of the Canaanite fertility religion. The Israelites had been warned not to engage in this abominable practice by Moses (see Deuteronomy ch.23 v17-18).

There were even male shrine prostitutes in the land; the people engaged in all the detestable practices of the nations the Lord had driven out before the Israelites. 1 Kings ch.14 v24

He expelled all the male shrine prostitutes from the land and got rid of all the idols his fathers had made. 1 Kings ch.15 v12

I will punish not your daughters when they turn to prostitution, nor your daughters-in-law when they commit adultery, because the men themselves consort with harlots and sacrifice with shrine-prostitutes. Hosea ch.4 v14

So what were they doing?
> No Israelite man or woman is to become a shrine prostitute.
> You must not bring the earnings into the temple of the Lord.
> Yet even some priests slept with the women slaves.
> Male and female prostitution was clearly available.
> Men went to the temple and slept with the women slaves.

God was very displeased with the practice. It broke away from the Mosaic law and it was clearly forbidden. God clearly removed all the Canaanite religion from the Promised Land in which the Israelites lived and settled.

But the kings and other officials still encourage the prostitutes. In the New Testament it was there in Corinth (see 1 Corinthians ch.7 v2-5). Corinth was characterised by Greek culture. One of the most famous temples in Corinth dedicated to Aphrodite, the goddess of love, whose worshippers practised religious prostitution.

When the Slave Goes Home

When all the Israelite slaves go free, it would be a moment of success, freedom and jubilation. The poor man who did not have any provisions would be released and go back to his home. When a person entered slavery, his master would take him far away, but in the same country of Israel or Judah.

So what did he find after six years?
> The place is dirty and no cleaning has been done at all.
> The place will be deserted and nobody would be there.
> The fields that he had were overgrown with weeds.
> He had money, but not enough to redeem him.

When you release him, do not send him away empty-handed. Supply him liberally from your flock, your threshing floor and your winepress. Give to him as the Lord your God has blessed you. Deuteronomy ch.15 v13-14

The master should supply the Israelite slave with all that he needs:
> Give him liberally from your flock.
> Give him the crops, the corn.
> Give him your wine.
> Give to him as the Lord has blessed you.
> Give to him that he needs to start again.

Remember, that's what the Lord God did for you when he released you from the hand of Egypt the land of slavery and dreadful, hard work.

There will always be poor people in your land. Therefore, I command you to be open-handed towards your brothers and towards the poor and needy in your land. Deuteronomy ch.15 v11

When the slave gets home, he can begin again. Sheep, seeds to sow and wine. It is not something that has to be done: one sheep, brushings from the threshing floor and one drink. But liberally, it means what he needs kindness and open-handedness. Something he has to do to keep him in the Promised Land.

He has to start again, but the Israelites would work together; one is rich but the other is poor, so the poor could make himself get rich again. All of them were brothers towards the Lord who created them.

Look upon my suffering and deliver me, for I have not forgotten your law. Defend my cause and redeem me; preserve my life according to your promise. Psalm ch.119 v153-154

This is what the freed slave must have felt moved as he started once again.

Freedom for a Slave

If a slave has taken refuge with you, do not hand him over to his master. Let him live among you wherever he likes and in whatever town he chooses. Do not oppress him. Deuteronomy ch.23 v15-16

This was a remarkable event. If a slave went across the boundary of Israel or Judah, he was safe from being handed back to his slave master.

Why was that?
> Slavery was Israel's past like the slaves in Egypt.
> God is looking at a slave and he was part of Israel.
> Nobody should hand the slave back to his master.
> If he wanted to live among God's people.
> He could pick his tribe and town.
> Do not oppress him, which means he would be our close friend.
> A brother and a sister in Israel.

God regards the poor in Israel, the alien, the fatherless and the widow. People who haven't the means for collecting the produce of the land. The husband might die and the widow would look after her children. What about the alien he would be pushed out of his country and come to Israel, what did he find?

When you are harvesting in your field and you overlook a sheaf, do not go back to get it. Leave it for the alien, the fatherless and the widow, so that the Lord your God may bless you in all the work of your hands. Deuteronomy ch.24 v19

It is the same practice, harvesting for the olives and the grapes.

- - - - - - - - - - - - - -

Boaz asked his foreman:

"She is the Moabitess who came back from Moab with Naomi. She said, 'Please let me glean and gather among the sheaves behind the harvesters'. She went out in to the field and has worked steadily from morning till now, except for a short rest in the shelter." Ruth ch.2 v6-7

The foreman would look after Ruth and he would know that she was working steadily. It was customary for the men to cut the grain and the servant girls to go behind them, to bind the grain into sheaves. Then Ruth could glean what was left behind. If they didn't do that and follow the principle, Ruth and Naomi would starve to death.

Slaves to be Bought

They wanted to go back to be slaves in Egypt. How little did they think about it? (see Exodus ch.2 v23)

The Lord will send you back in ships to Egypt on a journey I said you should never make again. There you will offer yourselves for sale to your enemies as male and female slaves, but no-one will buy you. Deuteronomy ch.28 v68

They didn't remember they were children growing up in the desert:
    They forgot God's laws and commands.
    They didn't see themselves as free.
    To go back to Egypt men and women as slaves.
    Not just one, but many and all of them.

Why is the Lord bringing us to this land only to let us fall by the sword? Our wives and our children will be taken as plunder. Wouldn't it be better for us to go back to Egypt? Then they said to each other. "We should choose a leader and go back to Egypt." Numbers ch.14 v3-4

Why did the people rebel against Moses?

They were exploring Canaan. Each of them were leaders (see Numbers ch.13 v3) to go, find out what the Promised Land was like, each tribe had one person, a leader going to look. What kind of land is it like? Are the people strong or weak? Few or many? What kinds of towns did they stay in? What is the soil like, is it fertile or not?

"We can't attack those people; they are stronger than we are." And they spread among the Israelites a bad report about the land they had explored. Number ch.13 v31-32

The leaders went came back and reported to the people that is why the people protested and moaned. It will be better to be slaves again.

- - - - - - - - - - - -

King Solomon was greater in riches and wisdom than all the other kings of the earth (see 1 Kings ch.10 v23), he had several slaves but they didn't satisfy him. He said, 'It was a chasing after the wind'.

I bought male and female slaves and had other slaves who were born in my house ... I became greater by far that anyone else in Jerusalem before me ... Yet when I surveyed all that, my hands had done and what I had toiled to achieve, everything was meaningless, a chasing after the wind; nothing was gained under the sun. Ecclesiastes ch.2 v7, v9, v11

More and more slaves, he didn't remember what he had achieved: houses, vineyards, gardens, parks, flowing water, herds and flocks, gold and silver, singers and a harem as well. But they didn't go home again after six years, they stayed and forgot what God had said in his law about slaves. It was abandoned under the Mosaic law they kept some, but ignored the rest.

- - - - - - - - - - - -

The wife of a man from the company of the prophets cried out to Elisha. "Your servant my husband is dead, and you know that he revered the Lord. But now his creditor is coming to take my two boys as his slaves." 2 Kings ch.4 v1

Even the prophets where not spared while they rented a house to live in. The creditor was coming to take my two boys as slaves. It was dreadful in Israel, they have quietly forgotten what God says in the law of Moses.

- - - - - - - - - - - -

As the years went on, the people of Israel still had idols to worship instead of the true God. They looked to see what the nations around them did and copied and imitated them. God said that in his law, 'The Israelites were taken away as captives away from the Promised Land' (see Deuteronomy ch.31 v29).

This is what the Lord says: "Was your mother sent away because I divorced her? Did I sell you as slaves to my creditors? No, you were sold because of your sins." Isaiah ch.50 v1 (NLT)

They had to learn being slaves again. Only a remnant of Judah came back to the Promised Land, the rest were left with the people there. It is a sobering thought.

So I handed her over to her Assyrian lovers, whom she desired so much. They stripped her, took away her children as their slaves, and then killed her. After she received her punishment, her reputation was known to every woman in the land. Ezekiel ch.23 v9-10 (NLT)

The Assyrian Empire was humiliating to the captives, the clothing was torn from their bodies. They didn't have enough to wear, they were exiled, chained to each other. Most people think that the Assyrian were cruel and dominated the land of Israel. It is true, you don't want the Assyrian Empire to take over your land.

Life or Death?

The Israelites went up from Egypt to the land that they were going to overcome and possess. They grumbled, complained and protested all the way along.

The Israelites said, "Why did you bring us up out of Egypt to this terrible place? It has no grain or figs, grapevines or pomegranates. And there is no water to drink!" Numbers ch.20 v5

Moses said at the end of his life, before the Israelites entered the Promised Land. He said, 'You will have two choices to make - life or death:'

"See, I set before you today life and prosperity, death and destruction. For I command you today to love the Lord your God, to walk in his ways, and to keep his commands, decrees and laws; then you will live and increase, and the Lord your God will bless you in the land you are entering to possess." Deuteronomy ch.30 v15-16

If they keep the words of God's law, the Israelites will never be slaves again. The words were forgotten and would be remembered no more. God's temple was not used again, the people thought that they were free and didn't sacrifice any animals. They busily got on with what they were doing. They were free but didn't realise that God was in control and he got them there.

- - - - - - - - - - - - -

While the Judges ruled the land.

The power of Midian was so oppressive, the Israelites prepared shelters for themselves in mountain cliffs, caves and strongholds. Whenever the Israelites planted their crops, the Midianites, Amalekites and other eastern people invaded the country. They camped on the land and ruined their crops all the way to Gaza and did not spare a living thing for Israel, neither sheep nor cattle nor donkeys. Judges ch.6 v2-4

If they followed God's commands there were no Israelite slaves at all. But sadly, after all these years both Israel and Judah were taken away as slaves again.Not by Egypt, but by the kingdoms of Assyria and Babylon. They forgot to follow the law of Moses, and didn't study it. It was forgotten while they feasted on the Promised Land and became rich and wealthy.

- - - - - - - - - - - -

When king Saul and the Philistines fought over the Promised Land. The formation of the kingdom of king Saul meant open rebellion against the Philistines. They formed up to protest about it. Goliath as a Philistine was a much feared, giant of a man, he shouted across the valley of Elah:

"Why are you all coming out to fight?" he called. "I am the Philistine champion, but you are only the servants of Saul. Choose one man to come down here and fight me! If he kills me, then we will be your slaves. But if I kill him, you will be our slaves! I defy the armies of Israel today! Send me a man who will fight me!" When Saul and the Israelites heard this, they were terrified and deeply shaken. 1 Samuel ch.17 v8-11 (NLT)

When they fought the victor could rule over the country of the loser. Take away the crops on his fields and most of the prized animals. It was desperate for the defeated, they would be slaves to the victor.

So David triumphed over the Philistine with a sling and a stone; without a sword in his hand, he struck down the Philistine and killed him. 1 Samuel ch.17 v50

- - - - - - - - - - - -

After the exile the slaves under the Assyrian and Babylonian empires were taken away, both Israel and Judah.

But see, we are slaves today ... Because of our sins, its abundant harvest goes to the kings you have placed over us. They rule over our bodies and our cattle as they please. We are in great distress. Nehemiah ch.9 v36-37

Though we are slaves, our God has not deserted us in our bondage. He has shown us kindness in the sight of the kings of Persia. Ezra ch.9 v9

They forgot the words of the Lord promised in Deuteronomy; the blessings and the curses. They are not willing to read and study about the king (see Deuteronomy ch.17 v14-20). Over the years, God sent the prophets to remind the people, but they simply ignored and persecuted them.

Stephen said in the Sanhedrin, "You stiff-necked people ... you are just like your fathers: You always resist the Holy Spirit! Was there ever a prophet your fathers did not persecute? Acts ch.7 v51-52

It should never have happened. Life or death, so the Israelites chose death.

The Nations Around Israel

So Joshua marched up from Gilgal with his entire army, including all the best fighting men. The Lord said to Joshua, "Do not be afraid of them; I have given them into your hand. Not one of them will be able to withstand you." Joshua ch.10 v7-8

God said, 'None of them will be able to fight against you'. The walls of the cities that they have to fight against were massive and the stones were immense. The men of the Nephilim were there, 'we seemed like grasshoppers in their sight'. God will be with you and take care of you.

Looking at the Israelites, we can see what they did:
> They didn't have iron chariots (Judges ch.1 v19).
> They made treaties with the people there (Judges ch.2 v2).
> They violated the covenant of the Lord (Judges ch.2 v20).
> To see and try their faithfulness (Judges ch.2 v22).

They were not fit to fight at all they were slaves, they were ordered around but they didn't really have weapons.

- - - - - - - - - - - - -

The angel of the Lord at Bokim and said, "I brought you up out of Egypt and led you into the land that I swore to your forefathers ... Yet you have disobeyed me. Why have you done this? I tell you that I will not drive them out before you; they will be a thorn in your sides and their gods will be a snare to you." Judges ch.2 v1-3

Israel didn't comply with God's commands: (see Deuteronomy ch.7)
> Make no treaty with them (v2).
> Show them no mercy (v2).
> Do not intermarry with them (v3).
> They will turn you away from following me (v4).
> To serve other gods (v4).

Break down their altars, smash there sacred stones (v5).
Cut down there Asherah poles (v5).
Burn their idols in the fire (v5).

Only the Lord could have overseen all of this trouble together with the people of Israel. He was mighty and strong, he removed most of the people of Canaan. For he remembered his covenant and he drove them out, he committed what he had said to Abraham long ago in the past.

- - - - - - - - - - - - -

What will happen to all of the natives or captives in the Promised Land?

Because of the sin of the Amorites has not yet reached its full measure. Genesis ch.15 v16

Suddenly they will be struck down. He will turn their own tongues against them and being them to ruin; all who see them will shake their heads in scorn. All mankind will fear; they will proclaim the works of God and ponder what he has done. Psalm ch.64 v7-9

God is very patient and kind. He will watch over the nations to see what they will do. He would remove the Canaanites together otherwise they will infiltrate the Israelites and remove God, worship idols and exercise sexual adultery.

- - - - - - - - - - - - -

They didn't drive all of them out. When the Israelites grew strong and able, but they left them there as slaves.

They did not drive the Canaanites out of Gezer, however, so the people of Gezer live as slaves among the people of Ephraim to this day. Joshua ch.16 v10 (NLT)

Later, however, when the Israelites became strong enough, they forced the Canaanites to work as slaves. But they did not drive them out of the land. Joshua ch.17 v13

(NLT)

The tribe of Zebulun failed to drive out the residents of Kitron and Nahalol, so the Canaanites continued to live among them. But the Canaanites were forced to work as slaves for the people of Zebulun. The tribe of Asher failed to drive out the residents of Acco, Sidon, Ahlab, Aczib, Helbah, Aphik, and Rehob. Instead, the people of Asher moved in among the Canaanites, who controlled the land, for they failed to drive them out. Likewise, the tribe of Naphtali failed to drive out the residents of Beth-shemesh and Beth-anath. Instead, they moved in among the Canaanites, who controlled the land. Nevertheless, the people of Beth-shemesh and Beth-anath were forced to work as slaves for the people of Naphtali. As for the tribe of Dan, the Amorites forced them back into the hill country and would not let them come down into the plains. The Amorites were determined to stay in Mount Heres, Aijalon, and Shaalbim, but when the descendants of Joseph became stronger, they forced the Amorites to work as slaves. Judges ch.1 v30-35 (NLT)

As God had said while the angel was at Bokim. They would fight against you.

- - - - - - - - - - - - -

When the Assyrian empire captured Israel, the people of the city of Tyre sent Hebrew slaves to Edom. Israel was helpless because of the Assyrians but Tyre broke the brotherhood, by letting the people go as slaves.

This is what the Lord says: "The people of Tyre have sinned again and again, and I will not let them go unpunished! They broke their treaty of brotherhood with Israel, selling whole villages as slaves to Edom. So I will send down fire on the walls of Tyre, and all its fortresses will be destroyed." Amos ch.1 v9-10 (NLT)

The people of Israel had been exiled from Jerusalem and the nations will be judged. They sold their people as slaves by casting lots for them. This is a malicious thing and its even worse about the Israelite children.

Edom is not like Assyria way up north. Edom is related to Esau, their brotherhood.

They cast lots to decide which of my people would be their slaves. They traded boys to obtain prostitutes and sold girls for enough wine to get drunk. Joel ch.3 v3 (NLT)

Israel would have been protected and nobody would be able to fight against it. It is only the sins of the Israelites that has forgotten and disregarded God's commands. God reminded the Israelites, "They will be a thorn in your sides and their gods will be a snare to you." Even today, there were Arabs among the Israelites whom God had chosen as his people. This scene goes on today the Arabs and Israelites, throwing missiles and bombs across the Promised Land.

A King for Israel

So all the elders of Israel gathered together and came to Samuel at Ramah. They said to him, "You are old, and your sons do not walk in your ways; now appoint a king to lead us, such as all the other nations have." 1 Samuel ch.8 v4-5

This greatly displeased Samuel but he prayed to the Lord. The Lord told him, 'Listen to what the people are saying to you. It is not you, but they have rejected me as their king. Tell them what the king should do'.

Samuel solemnly told them: (see 1 Samuel ch.8 v11-17)
>He said to make others to plough his ground.
>He said to make others to reap his harvest.
>He said to make others to make weapons of war.
>Your daughters are to be perfumers and cooks.
>I want the best of your vineyards and olive groves.
>He said I will take a tenth of your grain.
>Your sons, man servants and maid servants he will use.
>He said the best of your cattle and donkeys he will use.
>You yourselves will be slaves to him.

When that day comes, you will cry out for relief from the king you have chosen, and the Lord will not answer you in that day. 1 Samuel ch.8 v18

The people refused to listen to Samuel. They wanted a king to lead them out, like all the other nations, with a king to lead us and fight our battles. Saul a man of Benjamite, he was impressive, a man without equal among the Israelites, a head taller than any of the others. The Israelites chose a man without thinking that you will be his slaves. Nobody thought that after six years the slave could go home. It was a lifetime that the king's slaves should serve him and be subject to him.

God was really displeased. They had rejected God as their king and had even gone against his wishes that Israelite slaves had gone to join up to be the king's slaves. As a result, the law of God was quietly put aside people didn't read it. In God's temple they pushed it away silently, undisturbed. One book of the law of Moses. Most of the kings didn't read it; didn't even know it was around.

Over the years, the law of Moses was secretly put to one side, it was out of the way. Until Hilkiah the priest found it (see 2 Chronicles ch.34 v14-33). About 410 years from king Josiah to king Saul! Can you go back 410 years so what were you doing then? A few scraps of writing will be found, mostly records of violence and battles.

The king should read every day the words of his God follow carefully the words of the Mosaic law. When they became established in the Promised Land, the judges, the kings and rulers forgot. They passed it over to the priests to remind them. This was a dangerous path that they lived subsequently enemies came and all of the Old Testament was filled with the Israelites being over-run and outnumbered. This is the law of God. It will be seen in the Old Testament and the New Testament. God is unchanging, he is the same yesterday and in the future.

Abigail Becomes David's Wife

Nabal her husband of Abigail, treated David abominably. He was shearing sheep and this was a festive occasion (see 1 Samuel ch.25 v8).

There are a lot of sheep in the Bible. So in the spring when the lambs are born, we can have even two lambs for each mother. The shepherd watches over the sheep and they would graze on grass. He would be outside all-weathers protecting and keeping away lions and bears from the sheep. As summer comes to the end each year, they would be shorn to take away the wool and make it into blankets and fabrics.

David had about six hundred men with him and he looked after Nabel's sheep, he was wealthy and had three thousand sheep plus a thousand goats (see 1 Samuel ch.25 v2).

David said: (see 1 Samuel ch.25 v6-8)
When your shepherd we did not ill-treat them.
Nothing of theirs was missing.
Ask your servants and they will tell you.
David and his men became a protection around the shearers.
Please give to us servants at this festive time.

She was an intelligent and beautiful woman, but her husband, a Calabrite, was a surly and mean in his dealings. 1 Samuel ch.25 v3

Nabal replied: (see 1 Samuel ch.25 v10-11)
Who is this, David?
Many servants break free from their masters.
Why should I take my bread and water.
The meat I have given to my shearers.
Give it to the men who comes from where they were going?

He was in high sprits and very drunk. So she told him nothing until daybreak. There is the morning, when Nabal was sober, his wife told him all these things, and his heart failed him and he became like stone. About ten days later, the Lord struck Nabal and he died. 1 Samuel ch.25 v36-38

God struck Nabal and he died in about ten days. Nobody thought he was sick he was out with the sheep keeping watch over the shearers, he was in high sprits and drunk with alcohol which he kept. So Abigail went to David with a request.

She bowed low to the ground and responded, "I, your servant, would be happy to marry David. I would even be willing to become a slave, washing the feet of his servants!" Quickly getting ready, she took along five of her servant girls as attendants, mounted her donkey, and went with David's messengers. And so she became his wife. 1 Samuel ch.25 v41-42 (NLT)

She went to David and threw herself done before him.
She said:
> I would be happy to marry David.
> I would be like a slave to him.
> Washing the feet of his servants.

Abigail knew that Nabal was a horrible man, she recognised in David that he treated Nabal shearers honourably and respectfully. She understood that David would be king and she was incredibly bright. She was intending to be like a slave to serve him. Nabal's property in Carmel was very wealthy: sheep and goats and several fields came to Abigail but when she married David the property became his. David had a lot of children, the second of these was Daniel who was born to Abigail of Carmel (see 1 Chronicles ch.3 v1). The first of David's son was Amnon, but he was killed by Absalom (see 2 Samuel ch.13 v28-29).

Daniel should have been king over Israel, but God decided to select Solomon.

State Slavery

This was practised on a restricted scale by the kings David and Solomon.

David removed the crown from the king's head, and it was placed on his own head. The crown was made of gold and set with gems, and it weighed seventy-five pounds. David took a vast amount of plunder from the city. He also made slaves of the people of Rabbah and forced them to labour with saws, iron picks, and iron axes, and to work in the brick kilns. That is how he dealt with the people of all the Ammonite towns. Then David and all the army returned to Jerusalem. 2 Samuel ch.12 v30-31 (NLT)

There were still some people living in the land who were not Israelites, including Amorites, Hittites, Perizzites, Hivites, and Jebusites. These were descendants of the nations whom the people of Israel had not completely destroyed. 1 Kings ch.9 v20 (NLT)

These Solomon conscripted for his slave labour force, as it is to this day. But Solomon did not make slaves of any of the Israelites. 1 Kings ch.9 v21-22

Such use of war-captives was common though out the Near-East. The nations around Israel under the kings David and Solomon. But they didn't worry about the slaves at all they left them there, but they knew who they were.

We understand that David and Solomon after him were the best fighters in the land. They annexed all the nations and the land had peace for once. This was the only chance they had. To get Israel to learn the ways of God by avoiding slaves and letting the people serve the Lord. The questions of idols and sexual immorality were there in the people of Israel.

We understand that they didn't read and study the law of Moses. For example, to see what every king is supposed to do: (see Deuteronomy ch.17 v14-20).

He must be from among your own people, not a foreigner.
He should not pursue a great many horses.
He must not let the people go to Egypt where they were slaves.
He must not take many wives, his heart might be led astray.
He must not accumulate large amounts of silver and gold.
He is to write down a copy of the law of God and read it every day.
He is not to be considered better than all the rest of the people.

The kings picked and chose what they should do, regardless of the law of God and they had state slaves. If the kings David and Solomon had read the law every day, they would not have engaged with flippancy (thoughtlessness and disrespectfulness) as kings.

Slave Becomes a Prince

It is not fitting for a fool to live in luxury or for a slave to rule over princes! Proverbs ch.19 v10 (NLT)

A slave who becomes a king, an overbearing fool who prospers. Proverbs ch.30 v22 (NLT)

So what did the book of the Proverbs above say:
    A slave could never be king.
    A slave must eat poor food.
    A slave is a proud fool.
    A slave could even learn routine tasks.

Because of the nature of the book of Proverbs they made statements as to the young, to be able to, or how to behave. So, it is not the fault of a slave who is captured and made to work as a slave, like Joseph (see Genesis ch.37 v28 and Genesis ch.41 v39-40).

Such verses are generally true, but we have to remind ourselves that certain verses are not to be taken as literal. For example: (see the book of Proverbs)
    The years of the wicked are cut short (ch.10 v27), and
    The righteous live long and prosperous lives (ch.3 v2).
    The righteous will have abundant food (ch.10 v3), and
    The wicked will go hungry (ch.13 v25).

The Proverbs are indicating what the young should do and there is a lot to learn. It is a proverb to illustrate and make the situation clear.

- - - - - - - - - - - - -

Consider Daniel who was promoted above everything:

The Lord delivered Jehoiakim, king of Judah into his hand, along with some of the articles from the temple of God ... Then the king ordered Ashpenaz, chief of his court officials, to bring in some of the Israelites from the royal family and the nobility .... They were to be trained for three years, and after that they were to enter the king's service (in Babylon). Daniel ch.1 v2-3, v5

Wise men were instructed to give advice to the king. Whereas priests and prophets dealt more with the religious side of life. Wise men were concerned about practical and philosophical matters. It is important that in Babylon men would be trained to help with the king who had enormous power over several regions.

Better get the nobility of Judah to help with administering the king's terrain and division of land.

But Joseph and Daniel both being slaves, rose up to take command over the people.

Jeroboam I his Slaves

Jeroboam was a man of standing and when king Solomon saw how well he did his job, he put him to work in charge of the labour force of the house of Joseph (see 1 Kings ch.11 v28).

Standing: a reputation of status a position of authority and seniority. He required experience and he was going to do such a good task which king Solomon recognised.

Later, Ahijah the prophet of Shiloh wearing a new cloak met Jeroboam on the way. The two of them were alone out in the country. The prophet said to Jeroboam, 'I will give you the kingdom, because God has said that a tribe belongs to king David if you keep my statutes and commands' (see 1 Kings ch.11 v34-39). Ahijah took the new cloak he was wearing and tore it into twelve pieces. He said to Jeroboam, 'Take ten pieces for yourself'.

Jeroboam talked about the new kingdom but he shouldn't have done that. King Solomon heard about it and he tried to kill Jeroboam. But Jeroboam fled to Egypt and stayed there until Solomon's death (see 1 Kings ch.11 v40).

- - - - - - - - - - - -

After seeking advice, the king (Jeroboam) made two golden calves. He said to the people, "It is too much for you to go to Jerusalem. Here are your gods, O Israel, who brought you up out of Egypt." One he set up in Bethel, and the other in Dan. And this thing became a sin. 1 Kings ch.12 v28-30

Jeroboam didn't really trust God: He thought it was too much for the people. He sought advice from his council, rather than God. He created two golden calves and he was mindful of his sins and ignored the prophet who had told him what to do.

He forgot the first four Ten Commandments (see Exodus ch.20 v1-7) that God had provided for his people at the Mountain of Sinai:

I am the Lord your God.

You shall have no other gods before me.

You shall not make for yourself an idol.

You shall not misuse God's name.

- - - - - - - - - - - -

Jesus reminded the rich young man of the Ten Commandments in the New Testament (see Matthew ch.19 v17-19), about 950 years before king Jeroboam I. It is still to be used as a mark of respect and authority for God.

Because of this, I am going to bring disaster on the house of Jeroboam. I will cut off from Jeroboam every last male in Israel - slave of free. I will burn up the house of Jeroboam as one buns dung, until it is all gone. 1 Kings ch.14 v10.

That is why God said, 'I am going to bring disaster on the house of king Jeroboam I, even upon his slaves'.

Why?

God said, "Because you have provoked me to anger and have caused Israel to sin." 1 Kings ch.21 v22

Even the free persons and the slaves knew that king Jeroboam had done and nobody had a problem with what he had fulfilled and kept. They were happy to let the Israelites go off to the foreign, golden calves. They removed God presence and let the people do the same thing.

Captive a Slave Girl

Captives, especially prisoners of war were commonly reduced to slavery. A custom that goes back as far as written records, or even Noah.

I lift my eyes to you, O God, enthroned in heaven. We keep looking to the Lord our God for his mercy, just as servants keep their eyes on their master, as a slave girl watches her mistress for the slightest signal. Have mercy on us, Lord, have mercy, for we have had our fill of contempt. We have had more than our fill of the scoffing of the proud and the contempt of the arrogant. Psalm ch.123 (NLT)

Just as a servant girl looks to her mistress and what she wants. They presented themselves as humbly dependant upon God, but they couldn't do anything about the proud and the arrogant.

Now bands from Aram had gone out and had taken captive a young girl from Israel, and she served Naaman's wife. She said to her mistress, "If only my master would see the prophet who is in Samaria! He would cure him of his leprosy. 2 Kings ch.5 v2-3

Naaman was a commander of the king of Aram. He was a great, highly regarded and a valiant soldier. Through him, the Lord had given victory to the country of Aram but he had leprosy.

Leprosy: the topic of suffering and disease (was defined in Leviticus ch.13-14), but did embrace other skin conditions. Particularly for the diseases, the same is transferred to clothing and houses where they remained. Suffering is often ineffective and there would be a note of despair as they didn't have any treatments like we have today. The leper was cut off from his family outside the town where he lived slowly, the fingers and toes dropped off and the person could not have lived long.

- - - - - - - - - - - -

The prophet Oded said to Israel when it returned to Samara with a great deal of plunder and slaves:

But you have slaughtered them in a rage that reaches to heaven. And now you intend to make the men and women of Judah and Jerusalem your slaves. But aren't you guilty of sins against the Lord your God? 2 Chronicles ch.28 v9-10

There is no way that the slaves would go free after six years. It is all forgotten and the law of Moses is disregarded, for now. But the kings of Israel and Judah didn't read the law of Moses they required a priest to do it. But the priest was as bad as they were.

- - - - - - - - - - - -

Your sons and your daughters will be given to another nation, and you will wear out your eyes watching for them day after day, powerless to life a hand. Deuteronomy ch.28 v32

We cry to the Lord in heaven because we are slaves, like captives:
 We look to God for mercy and compassion.
 Just as we look to our slave masters.
 As a girl looks to her mistress for the slightest signal.
 We are full of contempt and the scoffing of the proud.
 The contempt of the arrogant.
 Who treat slaves like they are no good for anything?

Jeroboam II his Slaves

This was suffering at the power of the nations around them. A free Israelite was suffering harshness, cruelty and unhappiness in his life. It will be even worse for the slaves under the Israelite. The punishments by Moses has been forgotten (see Deuteronomy ch.28 v15-68) slowly and finally what God had said, 'Was indeed true'.

The Lord saw how bitterly every one in Israel, whether slave of free, was suffering; there was no one to help them. And since the Lord had said that he would blot out the name of Israel from under heaven, he saved them by the hand of Jeroboam son of Jehoash. 2 Kings ch.14 v26-27

The slave is worse than the free sons because he is bound to his master and has to do the work for him. The free sons can relax, independent in his master's house, but the slaves do all the work and they can't take it easy.

Jeroboam II he reigned in 785-749 BC:
 He did evil in the sight of the Lord.
 He did not turn away from the sins of Jeroboam I, son of Nebat.
 He rescued them from the son of Ben-Hadad (see 2 Kings ch.13 v25).

All because of the sins of the king who was responsible for the people under him. Particularly the sins of Jeroboam I, who selected golden calves to avoid the people going to the temple that God had selected in Jerusalem. We don't know much about the slaves, but Israel had crops, fields and houses in which the slaves worked. God was mindful of his people and didn't let the nations around them harm them. They had to remember their sins and what they have done by going after idols and forgetting God.

- - - - - - - - - - - -

Much later, What Stephen, a man full of grace and power, did great wonders and miraculous signs among the people, said when he was arrested in the Sanhedrin:

But God turned away and gave them over to the worship of the heavenly bodies. This agrees with what is written in the book of the prophets ... You have lifted up the shrine of Molech and the star of your god Rephan, and the idols you made to worship. Acts ch.7 v42-43

Before he was brutally stoned to death outside the city because he remembered that Jesus was the Christ. This was a missed opportunity to the Jewish leaders for they crucified him.

What did Jeremiah Say?

Jeremiah was a prophet who protested about the people in Jerusalem under kings Josiah, Jehoiakim, and Zedekiah. King Josiah, he reformed Judah, put the temple back in use and he celebrated the Passover. He didn't do enough to save the nation for under King Manasseh, he was indeed dreadful and wicked and the people followed him.

The last two kings of Judah didn't agree with Nebuchadnezzar, King of Babylon. Who inherited most of the Assyrian Empire and had armies which ruled the known world? The sons of king Josiah were more ambitious and Jeremiah could not curb their rash ambitions with his harsh warnings.

Is Israel a servant, a slave by birth? Why then has he become plunder? Jeremiah ch.2 v14

They would turn to God from their wickedness and humble themselves.

So you must submit to Babylon's king and serve him; put your neck under Babylon's yoke! I will punish any nation that refuses to be his slave, says the Lord. I will send war, famine, and disease upon that nation until Babylon has conquered it. Jeremiah ch.27 v8 (NLT)

He was the last prophet before the exile of Judah. He witnessed all the problems that the people had. He saw the Babylonian empire break down the walls of Jerusalem and captured all those who were marked to be slaves in Babylon.

He said, 'Before Jerusalem fell':

God said, "Every seventh year each of you must free any fellow Hebrew who has sold himself go you. After he has served you for six years, you must let him go free.

Your fathers, however, did not listen to me or pay attention to me." Jeremiah ch.34 v14

There were several difficulties among the people of Judah:
They had forsaken the Lord by idolatry (see Jeremiah ch.44 v1-6).
If you don't do it, you will be destroyed (see Deuteronomy ch.30)
The prophets had warned them continually (see 2 Kings ch.24 v2).
They failed to listen to what the Lord had said.

So all the officials and people who entered into this covenant agreed that they would free their male and female slaves and no longer hold them in bondage. They agreed, and set them free. But afterwards they changed their mind and took back their slaves they had freed and enslaved them again. Jeremiah ch.34 v10-11

Jerusalem was besieged. The siege was lifted for a short period following a rumour of the approach of the Egyptian army (see Jeremiah ch.37 v5), though it was immediately re-imposed. This was why the reason for the people to release these slaves it was not for the Israelite slaves at all. They didn't have the heart to do it while the city was surrounded by the Babylonians. After all, the slaves could do the work in the city.

- - - - - - - - - - - - -

Once the Israelites had fallen and the city was taken:

How deserted lies the city, once so full of people! How like a widow is she, who once was great among the nations! She who was queen among the provinces has now become a slave. Lamentations ch.1 v1

The people became slaves under the Babylon Empire; they were captured and taken away. In the summer of 587 BC the walls of the city were breached and Jerusalem was captured. A month later the Babylonians burned the city, including the temple and again many people were exiled to the city of Babylon.

"But you did not listen to me," declares the Lord, "And you have provoked me with what your hands have made, and you have brought harm to yourselves ... This whole country will become a desolated wasteland and these nations will serve the king of

Babylon for seventy years." Jeremiah ch.25 v7, v11

The whole region will become slaves for 70 years under the Babylonian Empire. The people had to die in slavery then the children will come back to the Promised Land once again. The land will have a rest to recover, there is no seventh year to let the land lie fallow.

In the first year of Cyrus king of Persia, in order the fulfil the word of the Lord spoken by Jeremiah, the Lord moved the heart of Cyrus king of Persia to make a declaration throughout his realm and to put it in writing ... Anyone of his people among you - may his God be with him, and let him go up to Jerusalem in Judah and build the temple of the Lord, the God of Israel, the God who is in Jerusalem. Ezra ch.1 v1, v3

Their children will go back to rebuild the temple and the wall under both Nehemiah and Ezra. This ends the Old Testament.

New Testament

In the New Testament it will be very different. The Roman Empire where slavery was justified and there was no room for ending the Jewish slaves once again. It will be a new beginning.

Care for his Slaves

When Jesus entered Capernaum, a centurion came up to him asking for help because he had a servant who was suffering at home. The servant or slave is paralysed.

But the officer said, "Lord, I am not worthy to have you come into my home. Just say the word from where you are, and my servant will be healed. I know this because I am under the authority of my superior officers, and I have authority over my soldiers. I only need to say, 'Go,' and they go, or 'Come,' and they come. And if I say to my slaves, 'Do this,' they do it." Matthew ch.8 v8-9 (NLT)

The faith of the centurion who had one hundred solders under him. He cared enough for his servant that he went to find Jesus. He commanded soldiers, servants and slaves he would be interested in them and what they were doing.

Jesus said to the centurion, "Go! It will be done just as you believed it would." And his servant was healed at that very hour. Matthew ch.8 v13

He astonished Jesus by his belief and his faith. Jesus remarked, that he had not found anyone who had such care for one of the centurion's people, even his servant or slave was troubling him.

Slaves are Less than their Masters

Jesus knowing that slaves would be there from the beginning to the end of the age. God created everyone as special, not as a slave working for his master, treated abominably and cruelly isolated from his home. Each one God made as unique, important and distinctive. He made all the creatures of the field, the birds of the air and the fishes in the sea, they obey mankind whatever his place in life, free or slave.

Jesus said, "Students are not greater than their teacher, and slaves are not greater than their master. Students are to be like their teacher, and slaves are to be like their master. And since I, the master of the household, have been called the prince of demons, the members of my household will be called by even worse names!" Matthew ch.10 v24-25 (NLT)

The situation was indeed unique, slaves like students will have to be taught. Otherwise, they would not know how the tools for their trade should be used.

Jesus reminded his disciples that the Pharisees called him the 'prince of demons'. But he was God himself, he said, 'You will be called worse names than that.' Jesus was saying that he himself was worse than any other son of their parent. The Pharisees didn't understand what they were saying, they thought that he was a devil and had to use the equipment that Satan had in his possession.

The slaves have to be taught to do what the master wanted. Everybody is different and the special apparatus or gadgets that slaves use were unique to what they were doing. Like the number of different forks, you could use to carry straw, dig the ground, empty a container and so on.

Jesus was Going Away

The coming of the Son of Man can be illustrated by the story of a man going on a long trip. When he left home, he gave each of his slaves instructions about the work they were to do, and he told the gatekeeper to watch for his return. "You, too, must keep watch! For you don't know when the master of the household will return—in the evening, at midnight, before dawn, or at daybreak. Don't let him find you sleeping when he arrives without warning. I say to you what I say to everyone: Watch for him!" Mark ch.13 v34-37 (NLT)

Jesus said:
> He was going away for a long while.
> He gave his slaves instructions for the work to be done.
> He told the gatekeeper to watch for his return.
> Watch! whether it is night or morning.
> Don't let him find you sleeping.
> Everybody should watch and wait.

The day and hour were unknown. Several people over the years have decided what it should be. They think that looking at the books of Daniel and Revelation gives us a clue but they are misled.

"No-one knows about that day or hour, not even the angels in heaven, nor the Son, but only the Father." Matthew ch.24 v36

They have forgotten the words that Jesus said, 'Only the Father, not even Jesus knew when he was going to return'.

The slaves would watch for that coming. Everybody should watch for the day, you don't want to be 'sleeping' and beat your slaves or ill-treat them. It is not the risk of sleeping when you are tired, but each day you watch and wait for Jesus to appear. It might be today! Don't get involved with evil plans that Satan has for you to do. Study the Bible, pray constantly and be committed to do the things that Jesus has commanded while he was here on earth. To often we get involved with things that might get your attention far away and be doing all the right duties. Jesus said, 'Just watch and wait for his coming.'

Slaves to Sin

Jesus replied, "I tell you the truth, everybody who sins is a slave to sin. Now a slave has no permanent place in the family, but a son belongs to it for ever. So if the Son sets you free, you will be free indeed." John ch.8 v34-36

In other words:
> Jesus was 'telling the truth'; he made it totally sure.
> Each and everybody who sins, fails to do what is right.
> They acted in error as God instructed or commanded them to do.
> Sin is doing wrong, speaking wrong and thinking wrong.
> We are a slave to sin and we cannot escape from it.
> A slave has no liberties and they are excluded from God's family.

However, if the Jesus sets you free, you will be free indeed. How can we escape from sin? We are programmed to sin and we will surely die (see Romans ch.5 v12). God had given Jesus as a sacrifice for sin (see Galatians ch.4 v4-5) it caused him to painfully suffer, die on a cross and be raised again. If you come to Jesus as Saviour and Lord and you are no longer a slave to sin, but a son of God, he has made you also an heir (see Galatians ch.4 v6-7).

- - - - - - - - - - - - -

Jesus prayed to his heavenly Father before he was arrested:

"I have brought you glory on earth by completing the work you gave me to do." John ch.17 v4

Jesus did not heal all the sick, perform great miracles, cast out the evil spirits that people had, or free slaves from captivity. He only completed his work that the Father gave him to do. It is important that you understand this. He was a Jew and it is only for the Jews located in Palestine. It is only three years that he was doing his ministry on earth. The Holy Spirit came on the people who knew Jesus, then the ministry started from Jerusalem to go into the whole world.

Jesus died for the whole world but the Holy Spirit came to teach everybody to believe. He is still going on working.

For Christ died for sins once for all, the righteous for the unrighteous, to bring you to God. 1 Peter ch.3 v18

On the cross Jesus died for the whole world, everybody and that includes you. Everybody has to come to receive him by faith in his work. It is a trusting, sure foundation. Regardless of what will happen to us here on earth, whether we are slaves or free.

We Must be a Slave for God

Jesus said, "Not so with you. Instead; whoever wants to become great among you must be your servant, and whoever wants to be first must be your slave - just as the Son of Man did not come to be served, but to serve, and to give his life as a ransom for many." Matthew ch.20 v26-28

Jesus became nothing in the eyes of the world and he gave his life up and went to the cross. As a ransom for many souls, including you.

Jesus was unequalled and one that is special:
He was born in a manger, not in a castle (see Luke ch.2 v7).
He was sinless, but not like us (see Hebrews ch.4 v15).
In him was life but we had darkness (see John ch.1 v4-5).
Jesus saw his Father but we didn't see God (see John ch.1 v18).
He knew he was going to die (see Matthew ch.20 v18-19).
He had peace, but the Jews rejected him (see Luke ch.19 v42).
He was frightened but he had to go through with his death (see Matthew ch.26 v38-39).

This is what Jesus did, for you:
He was divine.
He was the Son of God.
He had humility.
He was indeed a slave for us.
He died for us and rose again.
He ascended into heaven.

If you want to be great; first you must come as a servant and be a slave.

Anyone who does not take his cross and follow me is not worthy of me. Matthew ch.10 v38

For us to live in this earth we are bound by the fact that we will be following Jesus, regardless of what will happen. We may life a full life or be killed, that is what Jesus did. We will have to be a slave for God. Do you understand what that means? God directs and we follow Jesus, he decides and we must obey. God has a plan for us to work for him, he rearranges our lives to suit him. He chooses what we must do and our lives are in God's hands. God knows what we need. He understands that we might be frightened or nervous. For he is kind and considerate, he is trying to make us be heirs of his kingdom. He disciplines us to make us better.

He is God Almighty and we are not. We must be a slave to God.

Jesus was Crucified

Jesus became like us, made of flesh and blood. He did this, because by only dying could he rescue us from the horror of what is to come. God the Father knew that when people died, they were eventually judged and going to hell. Because of the sin that people carried around with them. The Father who is holy could not even exist with sin and therefore people would be alienated from God for ever.

Because God's children are human beings—made of flesh and blood—the Son also became flesh and blood. For only as a human being could he die, and only by dying could he break the power of the devil, who had the power of death. Only in this way could he set free all who have lived their lives as slaves to the fear of dying. Hebrews ch.2 v14-15 (NLT)

Jesus only died on the cross so that we could be saved. We have to trust in him as our Saviour and Lord. Be prepared to let the bad things go away and depart. We all have free will so God would be patient and knock loudly, but you will have to decide on your own.

Jesus had cried out again in a loud voice, he gave up his spirit. At that moment the curtain of the temple was torn in two from top to bottom. The earth shook and the rocks split. Matthew ch.27 v50-51

The curtain of the temple separated us from God. At that moment the curtain of the temple was torn in two from top to bottom. Jesus had sacrificed his life for all of us. He was raised again in three days by God and went back into heaven after returning to his disciples. His work was done. Now it is us and the Holy Spirit we pass on his message to the lost.

"Do not be afraid. I am the First and Last. I am the Living One! I was dead, and behold I am alive for ever and ever! And I hold the keys of death and Hades." Revelation ch.1 v17-18

Jesus went to the cross to save you and he holds the key to death and Hades. You don't really think that you are lost? Your soul goes on to God when you are dead and there is a waiting period in Hades before the judgement, where God separates the good and the bad.

While we are free or slaves, there is no difference between all of them. The slave can be free indeed by coming to Jesus as Saviour and Lord. He will enjoy the benefit of knowing that on this earth he will be a slave, but when it is past, he will enjoy for ever that he will be free again.

Jews can be Slaves

Persons who had been freed from slavery, or the children of slaves called 'freed slaves' or 'Freedmen'. Who didn't have only six years to be slaves in the Old Testament? 'Freedmen'. It was a lifetime as a slave in the New Testament, but it was unusual.

Stephen, a man full of God's grace and power, performed amazing miracles and signs among the people. But one day some men from the Synagogue of Freed Slaves, as it was called, started to debate with him. They were Jews from Cyrene, Alexandria, Cilicia, and the province of Asia. None of them could stand against the wisdom and the Spirit with which Stephen spoke. Acts ch.6 v8-10 (NLT)

Cyrene is the chief city in Lybia and North Africa, half-way between Alexandria and Carthage. One of its population groups was Jewish (see Acts ch.11 v19). Alexandria was the capital of Egypt and second only to Rome in the Empire. Two out of the five districts in Alexandria were Jewish. Cilicia a Roman province in the south-eastern corner of Asia Minor adjourning Syria. The freed slaves of the Jews began to argue with Stephen but he was truthful in what he said.

But they secretly persuaded some men to say, "We have heard Stephen speak words of blasphemy against Moses and against God." Acts ch.6 v11

Stephen declared that the worship of God was no longer restricted to the temple in Jerusalem; his opponents twisted his words to bring up an accusation that Stephen was attacking the temple, Moses by the law and ultimately God himself (see Acts ch.7 v48-50). It was a twisted version of what Stephen was saying.

The freed slaves were powerless to argue against Stephen whereas an accusation where Stephen was seized and brought to the Sanhedrin. The Sanhedrin saw his face was like that of an angel (see Acts ch.6 v15). They gave Stephen an opportunity to present charges. Eventually he said, 'You have killed and murdered Jesus' (see Acts ch.7 v51-53).

What did the Sanhedrin do?
>   They covered and protected their ears to not hear him speaking.
>   They were yelling at the top of their voices.
>   They dragged him out of the Sanhedrin.
>   They stoned him to death (see Acts ch.7 v58).

This was an opportunity for a great persecution broke out against the church at Jerusalem. The church was scattered from the city (see Acts ch.8 v1).

Slave who Predicted the Future

We were met by a slave girl who had a spirit by which she predicted the future. She earned a great deal of money for her owners by fortune-telling. This girl followed Paul and the rest of us, shouting, "These men are servants of the Most High God, who are telling you the way to be saved." She kept this up for many days. Finally, Paul became so troubled that he turned round and said to the spirit, "In the name of Jesus Christ I command you to come out of her!" At that moment the spirit left her. Acts ch.16 v16-18

This 'python' was a mythical snake, worshipped at Delphi and associated with the Delphi oracle. A 'python' spirit, a demonic spirit. The word 'python' came to be used through whom the spirit spoke. Since such persons spoke involuntary, as the demonic spirit gave them what to speak.

A slave girl who had a spirit:
> This young girl should not have been there.
> Who did what she was told by the Delphi oracle.
> She was there continuously, sweeping up or perhaps dusting.
> But the python spirit entered her.
> It was all to do with money for the slave owners.
> For the owners used her to speak what the 'python' said.

It is a warning that a very young girl, who was not married, had a demonic spirit who entered her and controlled her mind. That is a warning for us today, we don't worry much about our young children. Playing with Tarot cards, looking at witches on television, reading magical books, getting into the wrong evil of doubters. The evil spirit might have controlled more than one slave girl.

This might be looking for a child to enter, who didn't have any purpose in life.

Let the word of Christ dwell in you richly as you teach and admonish one another with all wisdom, and as you sing psalms, hymns and spiritual songs with gratitude in your hearts to God. And whatever you do, whether in word or deed, do it all in the name of the Lord Jesus, giving thanks to God the Father through him. Colossians ch.3 v16-17

Whatever you do, whether in 'word or deed', do it all in the name of the Lord Jesus should be the believer's hope for his family. It is important that you don't let your young children play with the magical arts. Even wizards and the like; keep them away from all that, watching the television, social networking and the books that they study or read.

All are One in Christ

The human body has many parts, but the many parts make up one whole body. So it is with the body of Christ. Some of us are Jews, some are Gentiles, some are slaves, and some are free. But we have all been baptised into one body by one Spirit, and we all share the same Spirit. 1 Corinthians ch.12 v12-13 (NLT)

In the church we are all one like in the whole body. So the two eyes can't stay in the same body, they see continually, where would we be without the eyes? For example: some of them are Jews and some of them are Gentiles. Some of them are slaves and some are free persons. It doesn't matter who are you, which way you are born and the way you live. There is no difference between the church elders and the church laity. It is the unity that binds us together with love (see John ch.17 v23).

This is a mistake that many church people grow to believe, even Christians. They think that the elders are special. The elders go to college and have special training and sometimes dress differently. But we are all the same, like in a whole body. The person in the 'eye' looks out and the person in the 'ear' hears, the person in the feet 'treads carefully' and the person in the stomach 'stretches'. There is no real difference at all. We are all separate from each other, but the body only exists if all the parts come together as one unit. Nobody has it all. Even the eye and ear; one sees but the other picks up sounds. This is why we are all needed and the body grows and expands together.

When Jesus will return, he collects all of his people and will join them in the air (see Matthew ch.24 v30-31). He will not say that the Anglicans are different from the Baptists, neither will he say that the Roman Catholics are different from the Methodists. They are all believers' parts of the body of faith. I understand there will be differences between them, like language. With dreadful, ham-stringing, man-made traditions. If they have come to the Lord as Saviour and Lord, they will receive the Holy Spirit and be part of God's family.

So you are no longer a slave, but a son; and since you are a son, God has made you also an heir. Galatians ch.4 v7

You are a not a slave, but an heir of God.

Believers are Not Slaves to Sin

As believers we understand that our 'old self' has been lost because we came to Jesus by faith in what he has done. We believe that his life, his death and resurrection has provided the way for God to approach us. We are going to have everlasting life when we die.

He who overcomes will inherit all this, and I will be his God and he will be my son. Revelation ch.21 v7

"For we know that our old self was crucified with him (Jesus) so that the body of sin might be done away with, that we should no longer be slaves to sin - because anyone who has died has been freed from sin." Romans ch.6 v6-7

When we come to the cross and believe in Jesus, we receive the Holy Spirit in our hearts and minds. We do not really understand this, but our 'old self' will be changed to produce the fruits of the Spirit; we will certainly be different.

You, however, are controlled not by the sinful nature but by the Spirit, if the Spirit of God lives in you. And if anyone does not have the Spirit of Christ, he does not belong to Christ. Romans ch.8 v9

The believer has the Holy Spirit within him or her. No question about it, it will be a change to our lives. The Holy Spirit will remind and rebuke us to be more like Jesus. Sin will still be there in our lives, so we have to come to the Father in heaven and say:

If we claim to be without sin, we deceive ourselves and the truth is not in us. If we confess our sins, he is faithful and just and will forgive us our sins and purify us from all unrighteousness. 1 John ch.1 v8-9

Jesus said, "Likewise every good tree bears good fruit, but a bad tree bears bad fruit

... thus, by their fruit you will recognise them." Matthew ch.7 v17, v20

This is what marks the people out who come to Jesus. It will be the Holy Spirit who will come into our lives and you will have to produce 'good fruit'. Your belief will change you and you will no longer be slaves to sin.

Slaves to God

We are not slaves to sin, but slaves to God!

Now that you have been set free from sin and have become slaves to God. Romans ch.6 v22

Shall we sin because we are not under law but under grace? By no means! Don't you know that when you offer yourself to someone to obey him as slaves, you are slaves to the one whom you obey - whether you are slaves to sin, which leads to death, or to obedience which leads to righteousness? Romans ch.6 v15-16

To explain the difference between them:
    When you came to Jesus.
    To let him be the Saviour and Lord of your life.
    You would be called, or noted as slaves to God.
    To let him be the master of all of your life.
    Where God wants, you must go.

The choice is yours. Either Satan or God. Whether you are slaves to sin which leads to death, or, slaves to obedience which leads to righteousness. We all are slaves to Satan, which means we do the wrong things every day, by word, by action or by thought. However, when we come to Jesus Christ as Lord and Saviour; we are freed from Satan and thereby we are slaves to God.

It is a choice we must make.

Billy Graham said, "If you are born in a garage that doesn't make you into a car." He was talking about from Satan to God. If you believe in God, or your parents were believers, or you went to church, or doing good things every day, even being a minister of the Word, that is not good enough. It's is like being in a garage, but it doesn't make you into a car.

Many Christians have not come close to the Lord. It is a surrender choice that you must make and not your parents or others who guide you.

You might recognise in your mind, but you must come to repent of your past deeds, believing that Jesus died for you and rose again. He wanted to be first in your life from now on. He is the master of your life and you will be slaves to God. Slaves to sin, or slaves to Jesus. Each one will be called a slave!

Slaves to Fear

For you did not receive a spirit that makes you a slave again to fear, but you received the Spirit of sonship. And by him we cry, "Abba Father." The Spirit himself testifies with our spirit that we are God's children. Romans ch.8 v15-16

We are special to God and that he gives us a visible sign that we are important to him by the Holy Spirit. It was a significant happening that we are sons of God, nobody could take that away from us. Whatever happens to us on this earth.

I consider that or present sufferings are not worthy compared with the glory that will be revealed in us. Romans ch.8 v18

We understand that sufferings and trials are here on this world but we are children of God. Do you know what that means? We are going to heaven when we pass from this earth; when we die. Think about it, how good is the God who chose us and selected us for ever!

Why are we not slaves to fear?

There is no dread or fear when we come to the Lord Jesus. For God so loved the world that he gave his only Son (see John ch.3 v16). I will be with Jesus, which is the most important thing (see Philippians ch.1 v23). We have the Holy Spirit within us to protect us and help us live this life which keeps us safe and guarded on this earth. Even Job who had a horrible time, but was protected by the Lord (see Job ch.1 v9, v12). It is by grace that you have been saved (see Ephesians ch.2 v5) not by any works, we will be God's own children, heirs to God.

Grace: this means the true salvation that Jesus redemptive work will achieve for all his disciples. A total well-being and inner-rest of spirit in fellowship with God. All true peace is Jesus' gift, a peace that lasts for ever.

Jesus said, "Peace I leave with you; my peace I give you. I do not give to you as the world gives. Do not let you heart be troubled and do not be afraid." John ch.14 v27

The place or the mind of the person has been cleaned-up but left unoccupied. (see Luke ch.11 v24-26). A reformed life but lacking God's presence is open to reoccupation by the evil spirits; it will be the worse to come. That is why God's Holy Spirit comes into the heart of the believer, it protects you from the enemy and all of his powers. It reassures you to not fear, whatever happens to you.

Onesimus a Slave

Paul probably wrote this letter and sent it to Philemon while he was a prisoner in Rome. He was imprisoned, chained up, waiting to be cleared once for all that, he had not gone into the temple in Jerusalem, associated with some people that were Greeks. He had been falsely arrested (see Acts ch.21 v26).

I appeal to you for my son Onesimus, who became my son while I was in chains. Formerly he was useless to you, but now he has become useful both to you and to me. I am sending him - who is my very heart - back to you. Philemon ch.1 v10-12

Onesimus one of his slaves had absconded, run away, which under Roman law was punishable by death. It was a dangerous task for he believed that Philemon had treated him badly. But Onesimus had met Paul and through his ministry had become a believer. Now he was willing to return to his master. Paul wrote this brief letter to explain and to ask that he be treated as a believer.

Perhaps this reason he was separated from you for a little while was that you might have him back for good - no longer as a slave, but better than a slave, as a dear brother. Philemon ch.1 v15-16

Confident of your obedience, I write to you, knowing that you will do even more than I ask. Philemon ch.1 v21

He was asking for the slave who ran away to be brought back to his master, not as a slave, but as a believer. Should he not have any slaves at all? What was he doing to ill-treat the slaves?

Yet, Paul did not explain his reasons:
He left it to Philemon to do what is right and proper.
How could a master and a slave be present at the Lord's table?

He was going to visit Philemon soon, as he was out of prison.
To see how the master and slave were getting on working together.

Slaves To Work Hard

Paul neither condones slavery nor any revolt against masters who had slaves. Rather he calls on both slaves and masters to show true principles of believers in their relationships. He thus attempts to change the slavery from the person within. Remember, that slavery was very common in the New Testament times. Everybody who was well off had slaves it was a Roman custom practised everywhere in the whole Roman empire.

The Holy Spirit will guide you not to have earthly slaves but will convince you that you are slaves to God.

Slaves, obey your earthly masters in everything; and do it, not only when their eye is on you and to win their favour, but with sincerity of heart and reverence for the Lord. Whatever you do, work at it with all your heart, as working for the Lord, not for men, since you will know that you will receive an inheritance from the Lord as a reward. It is the Lord Christ you are serving. Anyone who does wrong will be repaid for his wrong, and there is no favouritism. Masters, provide your slaves with what is right and fair, because you know that you also have a Master in heaven. Colossians ch.3 v22 - ch.4 v1

Most of Paul's letters were in the prison at Rome. Colosse had been a leading city in Asia Minor, but by the first century the city was diminished to a second-rate market town, because it had the neighbouring towns of Laodicea and Hierapolis, in power and importance (Colossians ch.4 v13). Most of the believers had slaves.

Does it mean that we can change?
    Slaves obey your masters not because you have to do it.
    With sincerity of heart since you are working and serving for the Lord.
    The Lord will give you a reward as a slave.
    Masters provide your slaves with what is right and fair.
    We should behave as believers.

Not to do what the world thinks and believes.
Or, what the Holy Spirit wants us to do.

That is what the society will mean: the rich and the poor, the added power of the wealthy and the miserably existence of the impoverished. The believers, whether slave or free can join together in God's church but they will certainly change with the Holy Spirit helping them.

Everybody is one in the body of the church.

All who are under the yoke of slavery should consider their masters worthy of full respect, so that God's name and our teaching may not be slandered. Those who have believing masters are not to show less respect for them because they are brothers. Instead, they are to serve them even better, because those who benefit from their services are believers, and dear to them. 1 Timothy ch.6 v1-2

Slaves will have to remind themselves that in society things will be changed as the body of Jesus grows and expands. In the church, slaves must consider their masters worthy of respect. To treat them better because they would be dear to them. This is the true sense of love. It is what Jesus meant by talking about the fruit, it must be different (see Matthew ch.7 v15-23).

It may mean the false prophets who went around prophesying, driving out demons, or many miracles. Jesus didn't know them, and they had it in their mind that they would be part of his family. False prophets were not welcome in God's family. They worked hard but only for themselves.

Slaves Respect your Masters

Both the Old Testament and the New Testament included regulations for slaves. Such regulations did not encourage or condone such situations but were given practical ways of dealing with the realities of life.

Slaves, obey your earthly masters with respect and fear, and with sincerity of heart, just as you would obey Christ. Ephesians ch.6 v5

Masters, treat you slaves in the same way. Do not threaten them, since you know that he who is both their Master and yours is in heaven, and there is no favouritism with him. Ephesians ch.6 v9

In the Roman Empire where slavery was established by law, some believers had slaves. Paul instructed them to honour both the slaves and their masters because they understood that there was a God who would be watching them.

There was no question about the slaves being freed under the Year of Jubilee in the Old Testament, they would be slaves for life. Not just under the Roman code, but slaves would be part of the normal activities of life for the rest of the world. It is not just an African slaves taken far away to work in the fields, but it was a current practice and it would be going on today. We don't talk about slaves, but we have them still there, even in England.

Jesus did not talk about all the slaves being freed. He had a mission from his Father in heaven to come to the Jews in Palestine, preach and teach them the truths, finally be sacrificed to help them come to God (see John ch.3 v16-17).

Jesus said, "It this world hates you, keep in mind that it hated me first. If you belonged to the world, it would love you as its own." John ch.15 v18-19

Jesus said, "But since you do not believe what he (Moses) wrote, how are you going to believe what I say?" John ch.5 v47

Jesus, God's own Son could not save the world as it was, there were far worse problems for the earth than slaves because of sin. Jesus would come to teach, preach and do miracles. But still the words 'hate me' will form a conclusion about what was it like for Jesus doing good to all. Even the crucifixion will cause some people to think what it was like for Jesus to be stretched out to die painfully, he was only a young man.

They gave him up to slowly die, even God's own Son.

Remember the Authorities

Think about the authorities who readily caused the slaves under the Roman government to be handed out and sold, most of the rich people had slaves. We know that if you are rich, you would have slaves as well. Otherwise, people will be talking about you, gossiping about it, asking why?

Remind the people to be subject to rulers and authorities, to be obedient, to be ready to do whatever is good, to slander no-one, to be peaceable and considerate, and to show true humility towards all men. Titus ch.3 v1-2

The importance of the authorities: be subject to rules and authorities and to be obedient. To be ready to do whatever is good and to slander no-one. To be peaceable and considerate and to show true humility towards men.

Why?

Everyone must submit to governing authorities. For all authority comes from God, and those in positions of authority have been placed there by God ... The authorities are God's servants, sent for your good ... They are God's servants, sent for the very purpose of punishing those who do what is wrong. So you must submit to them, not only to avoid punishment, but also to keep a clear conscience. Romans ch.13 v1-5 (NLT)

We must have a clear conscience and obey the authorities who were sent by God.

Once we, too, were foolish and disobedient. We were misled and became slaves to many lusts and pleasures. Our lives were full of evil and envy, and we hated each other. "But—when God our Saviour revealed his kindness and love, he saved us, not because of the righteous things we had done, but because of his mercy." Titus ch.3 v3-4 (NLT)

We too were foolish and disobedient.
We were misled and did things that are wrong.
We became slaves to Satan by sinning.
We acted with lusts and pleasures.

God revealed his kindness and saved us, not because of the works we had done, but because of his mercy. To let the authorities, keep the rules for our own good. Not because we don't think that they are right, they would be sent there from God himself. Who would stand up to God and say, 'We don't like the authorities in what they are doing?'

Slaves have a purpose to get things done. But because we all frequently sin, the correction God gives us is to try to make us to be slaves to God.

Whether we are free or a slave it doesn't make any difference.

Slave Traders and Law

We understand that the law is good, if one uses it genuinely and properly.

We also know that the law is good if one uses it properly. We also know the law is made not for the righteous but for law-breakers and rebels, the ungodly and sinful, the unholy and irreligious, for those who kill their fathers and mothers, for murderers, for adulterers and perverts, for slave-traders and liars and perjurers - and for whatever else is contrary to the sound doctrine that conforms to the glorious gospel of the blessed God. 1 Timothy ch.1 v8-11

Why is the law good?

God rescued the Israelites and took them out of slavery each one of them. Nobody could doubt that God did a wonderful thing by his miracles through Moses and Aaron and ejecting them out of Egypt to go to a Promised Land. Which he had promised to do by Abraham, this land is Israel's land and forevermore. After they left Egypt and went to Mount Sinai, God gave the Israelites the law of God through Moses. The Ten Commandments and the other laws to help them grow in faith, looking to the Promised Land. This is the law of Moses which reflects the duties of all the nations, tribes and peoples of the earth.

It all starts with recognising God in all his magnificence and power.

Jesus said, "If you want to enter life, obey the commandments." "Which ones?" the man enquired. Jesus answered, "Do not murder, do not commit adultery, do not steal, do not give false testimony, honour your father and mother, and love your neighbour as yourself." Matthew ch.19 v17-19

The Old Testament commandments should be the same as the verses in the New Testament. That is what God expected everyone should be doing. The Ten Commandments that God gave to Moses is the same as what we should be doing now. This is the basis for the 'Common Law' in the courts of justice in England.

Just as sin entered the world through one man, and death through sin, and in the way death came to all men, because all sinned - for before the law was given, sin was in the world. Romans ch.5 v12-13

'Before the law was given' meant that all men had to die because they sinned against God. If you break one of the Ten Commandments, you have broken them all. So that each person had to get old and die. Before the law and now.

For whoever keeps the whole law and yet stumbles at just one point is guilty of breaking all of it. James ch.2 v10

What is wrong with slave traders?

Slave traders took human slaves and gave them to another master. It was a go-between, they bought the slaves and passed them on. The money they earned added to the slave, the value for managing or handling each slave. If the slave died, they didn't worry or care. It was like a market for slaves and they didn't worry if the slave was ill-treated or beaten. The slave didn't have much clothing on, but that doesn't matter, all that the master wanted was to get the slave to work hard, doing a job different from what the slave had been doing regularly. If the slave was a doctor - but he would work out in the fields cutting corn. The past would not interest the slave trader. He cut corn.

It was a nasty business and wilfully forgotten what the slave meant to the Lord. He created each one personally, the slave is what he or he is doing on the earth; he or she was special to God and the Lord remembered him. If you are a slave, remember that God is watching you, he cares and loves you.

Ill-treatment of Slaves

You who are slaves must accept the authority of your masters with all respect. Do what they tell you—not only if they are kind and reasonable, but even if they are cruel. For God is pleased with you when you do what you know is right and patiently endure unfair treatment. Of course, you get no credit for being patient if you are beaten for doing wrong. But if you suffer for doing good and endure it patiently, God is pleased with you. 1 Peter ch.2 v18-20 (NLT)

What does it mean for the slave?
    Slaves must respect their masters and do what they tell you.
    If they are kind and reasonable, so well and good.
    If they are cruel and merciless, slaves can be beaten and die.
    When you suffer for what is right.
    Endure it with calmness and restraint.

God knows what you go through, he looks and considers what you do. If the master is fierce and vicious, gives you what is unreasonable work for you to do and beats you because you don't carry it through. The Lord will watch and will be pleased with you. God let the Israelites for 400 years in Egypt being ill-treated and badly beaten in a country not their own. He sent the Israelites away to go into exile for 70 years to Assyrian and Babylonian Empires because they forgot him and didn't serve him properly. They manufactured idols for gods.

He didn't forget them, he thought about his slaves and remembered them. After you have died, God will understand what you will have been going though and will comfort you and reassure you.

Remember Lazarus?

There was a rich man who was dressed in purple and fine linen and lived in luxury every day. At his gate was laid a beggar named Lazarus, covered with sores and longed to eat what fell from the rich man's table. Even the dogs came and licked his sores. Luke ch.16 v19-21

What happened?

The time came when the beggar died and the angels carried him to Abraham's side. The rich man also died and was buried: In hell, where he was in terrible torment; he looked up and saw Abraham far away, with Lazarus by his side. Luke ch.16 v22-23

God would leave you as a slave for this life, but he would welcome you for ever, this would be eternal life. As we go through this earthly life, many people will have to suffer, particularly those who are not well and have disabilities or even injuries. Even slaves who are badly treated and made to do impossible things.

Others were tortured and refused to be released, so that they might get a better resurrection. Some faced peers and flogging, while others were chained and put in prison. They were stoned; they were sawn in two; they were put to death by the sword. They went about in sheepskins and goatskins, destitute, persecuted and ill-treated - the world was not worthy of them. They wandered about in desert and mountains, and in cave and holes in the ground. These were all commended for their faith, yet none of them received what had been promised. Hebrews ch.11 v35-39

Not slaves, but the rest of God's family who stand up and tell the world what God really wants them to do, accepting Jesus as Saviour and Lord. They would be punished and ill-treated by the authorities and businesses. They maintained a commendation for their faith, but not in this world. They will expect God's kingdom to grow and not waver for their short life on earth.

The Conclusion

In the later days when God punished the nations, there was a great earthquake it was frightening and terrible. The sun and moon, the stars and every mountain and island were removed from the place where it stood firm.

Then all the kings of the earth, the princes, the generals, the rich, the mighty and every slave and every free man hid in caves and among the rocks of the mountains. Revelation ch.6 v15

Even the slaves at the end of time were there.

The beast out of the earth came from Satan: (see Revelation ch.13 v16-17)
> The beast forced everyone.
> Small or great, rich and poor, free or slave.
> To receive a mark on his right hand or on his forehead.
> So that no one could buy or sell unless he had the mark.

This is the moment that God had decided to end the time on earth.

They were scared by the intense heat and they cursed the name of God, who had control over these plagues, but they refused to repent and glorify him. Revelation ch.16 v9

On the earth they were scared and cursed the name of God. They forgot the Ten Commandments in repentance:
> I am the Lord your God.
> You shall have no other gods before me.
> You shall not make yourself an idol.
> You shall not misuse the name of God.

Only be careful, and watch yourselves closely so that you do not forget the things your eyes have seen or let them slip from your heart as long as you live. Teach them to your children and to their children after them. Deuteronomy ch.4 v9

Now the earth was corrupt in God's sight and was full of violence. God saw how corrupt the earth had become, for all the people of earth had corrupted their ways. Genesis ch.6 v11-12

Watch carefully!So that you don't end up like those who refused to repent. God is watching and waiting; several centuries have come and gone but God still waits, looking for his persons to enter his kingdom. The earth is dreadful place and it will get worse not better, the animals will still suffer and die. God still waits looking for you to repent and trust in Jesus as Lord and Saviour. Then you can turn from your evil ways and give the slaves back their freedom, this is what the slaves desperately desire or depend on; they want to have their lives back, to be free and not to suffer for the mighty and rich.

www.ingramcontent.com/pod-product-compliance
Lightning Source LLC
Chambersburg PA
CBHW051535120626
46551CB00012B/1235